RECRUITABILITY

A strategic job-hunting guide with the inside scoop from a recruiter

NIKKI NIEMCZYCKI

D1739292

CONTENTS

Free Bonus Gift

In addition to this valuable book about job seeking, I've created a free downloadable workbook to aid with your job search!

Simply click the link below (eBooks) or type this URL into your browser (paperback books) for access to the free Recruitability workbook

www.nnpublishing.com/free-gift

Introduction

There's nothing like jumping into a new position, whether you're just starting out in your career, or making a change. Beginning a job is a great way to develop new relationships, gain valuable skills, discover what you're passionate about, and boost your confidence! But let's be honest, the job seeking process itself can be challenging, time consuming and frustrating. The pandemic started an unprecedented shift in the job market that we live in today. People are not merely seeking employment, but rather making conscious choices to position themselves into careers that they'll enjoy. Careers that provide fulfillment, happiness, better overall options for their lifestyles and families, and a sense of pride for work that they do. Job opportunities are no longer tied concretely to locations either, which opens a world of possibilities for job seekers no matter where they live. On top of that, the state of our economy constantly shifts, which directly impacts employment rates, layoffs, and the rise and fall of demand for various types of talent.

The hiring process itself, while it has evolved over time in some regard, still follows a standard pattern, one that is quite similar to starting a new relationship. Job seekers and employers discover each other through means of digital channels, personal networks, and third-party tools and platforms, they conduct a two-way evaluation process, and ultimately choose to commit to each other. But with thousands of job listings available online, how do you navigate the chaos? Where do you start? How can you maximize your time to ensure your job seeking process is efficient? When you do find a match, how do you know you've found the "right one"?

This guide will provide you with some unique methods for job seeking, outside of the traditional online job search. Strategic and systematic methods that are tailored your specific goals. Along the way you'll learn how employers seek talent, and how to best position yourself to those prospective employers. This lens comes from ten years of recruiting and talent acquisition experience within various types of organizations.

You'll begin your search by learning how to break down and categorize the essential elements that make up a career choice and prioritize them based on your interests and goals. From there you'll learn several different approaches to job seeking, that allow you to capitalize on job opportunities that are most likely to match your requirements. Each chapter includes valuable inside information from the employer and/or recruiting perspective. When you understand how job seekers are evaluated from the other side of the fence, your job search will be more strategic, thoughtful, and effective. You'll also gain in-depth information about how to research companies and positions, which digital platforms are available and how to use them, and how to approach your resume, applications, interviews, and offers. On top of it all, you'll have several examples of verbiage you can use in your resume or social profiles during your search, questions to ask, and negotiating tactics. There's even a chapter dedicated to the process that recruiting and hiring teams use when seeking new employees.

If you're seriously considering making a change, or diving into the job seeking world for the first time, being informed and prepared will make the process come naturally. After reading this book you'll have a game plan for your job search, as well as a new sense of confidence when interacting with prospective employers. Enjoy!

Chapter 1

My Story

I'll admit, this first chapter was actually the last chapter I added to this book before publishing. This job-hunting guide is shorter than most non-fiction business books for a reason. I am a firm believer in sharing information in the clearest, most direct way possible. It didn't seem necessary to fill pages with "fluff" and tell my personal story or blabber on about my life. After all, this book is all about you! But as I started writing the content, I found myself reflecting not only on my career experience as a recruiter, but my own job-hunting journey as well. Furthermore, I realized that after interviewing over 5,000 people, I had heard so many career stories and methods that ended up inspiring my own career path. This chapter aims to reveal a real-life story of career twists and turns, trying different methods and approaches to job seeking, and lessons learned.

FINDING MY NICHE

I started college with no real idea of exactly what I wanted to do. I was a pretty good student, but like many 17- or 18-year-olds, I didn't really feel passionate about any particular subject or discipline. So, I went with a basic business major and started taking prerequisites, along with some business courses. I even joined a freshman-only, professor-led business club. We had weekly meetings where we discussed various types of business careers, how to conduct a business meeting, how to network in the business world, etc. The club also required business professional attire, and I was not into it. Call it youth, ignorance, or plain old stupid, but the dress code and the nature of the meetings made me feel like I was part of a dog-and-pony show. There was probably an unquantifiable amount of valuable business knowledge I could have acquired by staying in that club, but it didn't feel like me. I had trouble connecting with others in the group and didn't really see myself thriving in that kind of community or culture.

I quit the club, and continued with standard freshman courses across math, science, english, social sciences, and a few others to add some flavor to the mix. I always felt comfortable with public speaking, so I took a public speaking class my second year. I was still unsure of my degree, trending towards something in communications or liberal arts, but I had no set plan in place. I sat next to this one classmate, who I really got along with. We had a similar approach to public speaking projects, and I always found his speeches interesting and engaging, and vice versa. We ended up working on group projects together as well. This natural connection and respect for each other's work felt like true comradery, more than I ever felt in my business club. One day we talked about our majors, and I was vulnerable in disclosing that I had no idea what I really wanted to do. He simply told me "My major is graphic design, it's pretty cool, you should try it". I had no knowledge of the creative industry outside of some art and pottery classes in high school. But I figured, I have a ton in common with this person, we think similarly, we communicate similarly, and we've teamed up on projects that produced successful results. If he's good at it, and enjoys it, maybe I will too. I ultimately decided on a major from a gut feeling, rather than choosing something I knew was a strength of mine, and I loved it! I started diving into design courses, color theory, user interface design and web development, layout, typography, and some traditional art classes like drawing and painting. Turns out I was a pretty decent creative, and I also took some art history classes that sparked a lifelong interest in travel and culture.

Towards the end of my college years, I was feeling a little bit lonely as many of my close friends had either graduated or switched schools. I was also struggling to snag any internships, despite applying to dozens, and was worried I'd have a hard time landing a job after school. One evening, I was moping over a plate of chicken fingers at the local TGIFridays bar, when I struck up a conversation with an older woman sitting beside me. Even though I wasn't in the best of moods, I was always a very social person, so I was receptive when she engaged me in chit chat. We got on the topic of school, so I told her a bit about my path and that I was nearing graduation and didn't have a game plan for afterwards. After 30 minutes or so I discovered she was the head of my university's Office of Continued Education. Our conversation established a personal connection, which led to a fruitful result. She invited me to a formal meeting/interview on campus, and after a portfolio review, she offered me a

PAID internship for 10 hours a week as a graphic designer! This was a major break for me. Real, professional experience in my field of study. Until then my job experience consisted of retail, waitressing, and bartending gigs. Looking back now, I see how powerful networking was for my career. Without that interaction, I may have graduated without the internship experience, which was essentially a prerequisite for my first job out of college.

EARLY CAREER

There I was, a recent grad with a BA in Graphic Design and one internship under my belt. I got a tip from a professor about a junior design role with a sports and entertainment company, but it was only part time. Most graduates were looking for full time positions, so they didn't exactly have a ton of applicants. I jumped at the chance and landed the role. I learned a lot about professional basics like email communication, project documentation and structure, problem solving, and how to receive feedback. It wasn't paying the bills entirely, so I supplemented my income by doing some marketing and social media for a small business. My real goal, an industry that I learned about in school and was passionate about and inspired by, was advertising. I probably applied to 100 different advertising agencies between my last semester and 6 months post-graduation. I think I only received 2 interview requests, and sadly didn't get the job. Finally, after nearly a year of applying, I landed a role with a mid-sized advertising firm, 15 minutes from my home. It was perfect! I was finally going to work in advertising. A dream job that would allow me to express my creativity and change the world one brand at a time.

Well, it was far from that. I was the "junior" hire and found myself spending hours per day on what I guess you could call grunt work. I was a Production Artist, so I reformatted other people's work, prepared design documents according to specifications, made copy edits, and prepared mood boards and presentations to aid the creative teams with their epic brainstorming sessions. Over time I learned a lot and started to pick up some more true creative work. I was starting to design from scratch, take on solo projects, and contribute more to conversations. After building rapport with some of my senior coworkers, I asked about their career paths and what steps they took to get there. I also started researching typical advertising career progression, and standard organizational structures within agencies. After learning more from coworkers and my online research, and a couple of years in the agency, I was feeling a bit discouraged. An advertising career path seemed like a long, hard road, to get to work on exciting brands and make the big bucks. And on top of that, my office environment started feeling very political and gossipy. I felt slightly trapped in a system that there was no way to bypass, without putting in years of grunt work and playing the political game. I felt like I didn't have much control over my career path, and I began to crave something more entrepreneurial. This was quite ironic, as a few years earlier I quit a business club in pursuit of a life as a creative.

Regardless, I wanted to explore other routes. I wanted a career where I could grow financially and knowledgeably. I wasn't afraid to put in hard work, but I wanted to learn quickly and excel even faster. Something I enjoyed, but also allowed for rapid rewards with the right perseverance and commitment to excellence. So I hopped back online and started a job hunt. This time, instead of going after advertising agencies, I researched jobs that would be considered peripheral to advertising, or at least something that might be a good segway. I applied to some positions in marketing, communications, and sales. They all seemed to have a wider spread of career paths than the industry I was in. Specifically, I looked at the total number of Director or VP positions posted in these three fields and compared them to the number of Creative Director advertising positions out there (which is kind of the pinnacle of an advertising creative career). Now obviously I wasn't applying to Director or VP roles with my limited experience, but the drastically higher number of opportunities in those fields made me feel confident that they would be a good pivot.

One of the positions I applied to was with a staffing firm which specialized in the creative, digital, and advertising industries. It was a sales role, and they indicated that previous advertising experience was paramount, while sales was not. I landed an interview, and since I had no sales experience, and it wasn't a creative role, I just led with my knowledge of the industry and tried to display as many valuable soft skills as possible. Everyone I met with was impressive, yet approachable. It almost felt like the perfect blend of business acumen, and a relaxed agency-like culture. After a few rounds of interviews, they called to offer me a job (yay!) but they said, "We like you, we want you, but we think you'd be better in a recruiter role instead of a sales role, are you open to that?" Recruiters had an uncapped commission structure, similar to the sales hires, and I loved the idea of maximizing my income simply by learning how to be great at my job. I accepted.

THE STAFFING SAGA

Little did I know then, but I would spend the next 8 years of my career at that company. I like to call this part of my life "The Staffing Saga". For those who are unfamiliar with staffing, here's a brief overview. Staffing agencies operate as a third-party vendor, who work on behalf of a client to source, recruit, phone screen and submit potential candidates to their open positions. Staffing agencies are typically contingency based, meaning clients only pay them for service if they end up finding the right candidate for their role. Some firms work on full time direct hire positions, some do contract and hourly roles, and some do both. I'll explain more about staffing agencies later in this book, but what this created for me was an opportunity to learn what hundreds of different companies look for when hiring. And I learned a ton about the different roles and responsibilities that exist within their teams.

Recruiting came naturally to me, mostly because I liked to talk, I liked to listen to people's stories, and I had a good sense for personality alignment - or professional matchmaking if you will. And my industry experience definitely helped. Even though I never became a Creative Director, or a VP of Marketing, I had enough industry knowledge to navigate conversations with these professionals and ask meaningful questions to uncover their strengths. I was able to help many of these folks find new careers and learned a ton along the way. The more people I interviewed, the more I learned about digital marketing, content, advertising, UI design, digital products, brand strategy, B2B, B2C, art direction, photography, web development, user experience, and everything in between. Interviewing people quickly became my favorite part of recruiting. I was a sponge. I felt like I had the knowledge and career experience of thousands of different people stored in my brain. While I'd never claim to be qualified to do those roles myself, I could hold my own in conversations around any of those topics. I maintained some high success rates as a recruiter in terms of filling positions and providing good candidate experience to the people I interviewed.

I ended up becoming a trainer for other recruiters, opened two brand new branch locations, and contributed to company-wide task forces aimed to improve enterprise operations. I also established close, trusting relationships with clients. The more I worked with clients the more I enjoyed client interaction and began to uncover other needs they might have that our company could assist with. I began to feel a familiar itch for change, and after speaking with a few leaders I decided to try my hat on the sales side. I knew sales would be challenging, but I was confident in my ability to do the job and my manager supported me as well, so I went for it! I also knew that I could potentially grow my commission and overall income by killing it in sales, and figured having some sales experience could help me in the future should I choose to move to a new company.

Sales was hard, really hard. I felt like I had mastered the art of recruiting in a staffing environment but starting from scratch and introducing our services to clients proved to be much more difficult than I expected. It wasn't because I was uncomfortable talking to clients, or that I didn't know our capabilities in and out, I certainly did. But my manager and higher up leaders had so much confidence in me that I really wasn't given much support outside of some initial sales training. What I mean by that is they assumed I would be able to deliver the same results as a tenured salesperson, versus a newbie starting out in sales for the first time. Now don't get me wrong, I certainly had many amazing salespeople I could turn to for help and advice. But the actual list of clients that I had to go after, was frankly nothing more than the leftover scraps of the client database, or clients that had proven to be extremely difficult to contact or work with.

Essentially, I was handed a blank slate, no warm leads, and not much room in my market to expand, as most of the clients were already owned by other sales members. This isn't extremely uncommon for sales roles, so I'm by no means bashing the company that I worked for. But it taught me a valuable lesson about starting a new role. Even if you've been in a certain industry or company for an extended period of time, you have to take the time to ask what you will be provided with, how you'll be supported, and what will be expected of you. I dove headfirst into deep water with excitement, and nearly drowned because I wasn't equipped with the right knowledge. Looking back, I may not have made the decision to shift into sales, had I known how hard it would be to start again from the ground up. Regardless, I got on my grind and slowly but surely started pulling in some clients and contracts.

My company began to offer slightly different services as well. Rather than simply filling open positions, we began to offer managed services. This was quite different from the traditional staffing model. Instead of contingency based searches and staff augmentation, we were selling complete teams of individuals to do a specific project or scope of work, and we guaranteed the delivery of that work for a set price. I fell in love with this model, and it seemed to attract many more clients and potential partnerships than the staffing services I was selling before. My commission was beginning to creep up to the level I saw as a recruiter. Even though I didn't love the job, I would at least get back to where I was financially a year or so prior. I had already grown accustomed to that level of income, and I felt strongly that it was one of my biggest priorities.

Unfortunately, as soon as I started making progress, COVID 19 hit. The whole world seemed to go on pause. Not only did companies stop paying for third party services (like the one I worked for), but massive layoffs were taking place left and right, including my own company. Thankfully, I survived a 20% companywide layoff, which I assumed was largely due to my tenure. I certainly wasn't a top performer who was bringing in the big bucks in comparison to other sales employees. I scrambled to continue to sell, but I knew deep down it was yet again time for a transition. This time it wasn't about what I wanted to do, or for a change of pace, but rather what the world and the market was demanding. I knew I had to seek out something that would provide me with job security that would survive and thrive in a pandemic. I thought about what peripheral industries were close to marketing, design, digital and creative, and landed on technology as a good transition. I had no experience in IT recruiting or sales, but I knew a decent amount about the industry, as many of the teams I supported worked hand in hand with IT.

So I began my job search, again. This time around, I was specifically targeting technology and IT companies, and applying for both recruiting and sales roles since I now had a broader range of skills and experience. This was by far the longest and most grueling job search I experienced in my career. The list of available jobs was short, and I quickly realized that my 8 years in a staffing agency put me into a bit of a pigeonhole. Another lesson learned, staying in one industry too long can sometimes present challenges when looking to transition into something different. There's nothing wrong with company loyalty, strong tenure is impressive, and it says a great deal about your value at that company. But unless you plan to be in the same role for the rest of your career, make sure you're taking on new challenges, expanding your skills, and learning some other part of the business.

Many technology companies wouldn't even consider me for an interview because I didn't have IT experience. And others rejected me because staffing as a third-party partner is different from working internally within a corporation, or "on the client side". I was shocked by this. I knew next to nothing about many of the industries I worked in when I first started, but I was able to learn quickly and gain a deep understanding which ultimately led to success. I had a hard time trying to articulate this on a resume, I just needed someone to give me a chance in the IT world! Sadly I learned that getting past the "recruiter screening" process was tougher than I thought it would be. After many failed attempts, I adjusted my resume. I wrote detailed descriptions of the types of projects and big wins that I had across my career, backed with data and statistics. I included extra context around the managed services focus from the past few years. Managed services was more relatable to large corporations than staff augmentation was, and it showed that I was capable of more than traditional staffing services. Simultaneously, I researched companies that provided managed services or IT services with a technology lean. I found several IT services and management consulting firms that seemed to be the perfect transition for me.

After a couple of applications, the detailed resume proved successful! I landed some interviews and was able to have fruitful conversations with both recruiters and hiring managers. Some went well, but I kept coming in as the runner up against other candidates with more relevant experience. After my job pipeline ran dry, I turned to LinkedIn and looked up IT services and consulting firms in my local area. I found recruiters and HR employees at each firm and sent them personalized messages about my interest in the industry and desire to be considered for any openings that come up in the future. It took three months before I got a response, but finally an HR contact got back to me. She told me they didn't have the position posted yet, but they were looking for a Recruiting Manager and asked if I'd be open to a management role. I had never been a people manager before, but I was a trainer and a lead for years, so I felt totally confident I could take on more responsibility. I was a little nervous about how to answer management questions though, since I hadn't done that before.

I went through three rounds of interviews and connected well with everyone I spoke with. However, in the final round, I really blew it. I was totally unprepared for some of the questions such as how to manage team performance, how to hire and build teams, and how to scale a rapidly growing organization. Turns out I really wasn't qualified for that role, due my lack of management experience, and exclusive knowledge of staffing models verses corporate models. They gently let me down, but also mentioned that they were going to pivot to looking for a VP level talent acquisition professional instead of a recruiting manager. Clearly, they needed someone with more experience supporting a business from a leadership perspective, and that just wasn't me…yet.

Fast forward a few months later, I saw the same company post a job for a Recruiter role. Even though I had already progressed from a recruiter, to a senior recruiter, to a lead recruiter in the past, I applied. I figured taking a step back to get into the right industry, might pay off in the long run. I landed an interview again, this time with the man who now held the title VP of Talent Acquisition. Rather than try to hide the fact that I literally interviewed for his job a few months before, I brought it up right away. I simply made light of the situation and reinforced my interest in the recruiter position on his team. I wasn't a diva, and I didn't care about titles. I wanted to learn a new industry and I needed someone to give me a chance. We totally hit it off and genuinely connected on a personal level. A few weeks later, I received an offer! It wasn't great, it was a large step back for me financially, but I also understood the company was assuming some risk by hiring someone without all the IT experience they were looking for.

Before I accepted, I thought back on my past mistakes. I needed to get a crystal-clear picture of how I'd be supported, what growth opportunities existed, potential timelines for promotions and raises, and what would be expected of me in the first 30/60/90 days and first year. The hiring manager was patient and walked me through everything. I also just really, genuinely liked him as a person, and knowing I'd be reporting to him directly, made me confident that this was a good move. I had completed nearly 25 interviews at this point and most conversations felt robotic and scripted. While everyone at this company felt real, authentic, and down to earth. I knew that kind of culture was one I could thrive in, and I started my new role as a technical recruiter for an IT services consulting firm.

A WHOLE NEW WORLD

I was thrown right into the deep end. The only other recruiter at my company ended up going on maternity leave three weeks earlier than expected. With barely any training under my belt, I was essentially responsible for 100% of the recruiting and hiring for three to four months. I had to learn fast and grind every day, but my hard work paid off. My crash course led me to a very successful first year. Not only did I learn IT, but I absorbed a whole new world of talent acquisition that I hadn't been exposed to before. Before this role recruiting was all about matchmaking, a one-to-one pairing of the right person for the right role, based on a predefined qualifications. Now working in-house, I learned about quarterly and annual hiring forecasting, business needs, and projected growth. I was more deeply integrated with onboarding processes, HR procedures, equipment for new hires, and evaluations of recruiting processes to ensure talent acquisition was successful. We constantly reviewed and improved recruiting functions including: market research, sourcing and attracting talent, employer brand strategies, interview rubrics and evaluation methods, compensation and benefits benchmarking, candidate experience, and KPIs that measured the success of our department. I realized talent acquisition wasn't simply about filling positions. When talent acquisition is done well, backed by market research and data driven strategies, it is an essential operational unit for any business to scale their employee base in a healthy, long-lasting way.

Several changes happened over the years, including an acquisition by a much larger global company. Even though the acquisition was challenging, I was excited about the expanded opportunities for growth that a bigger company would provide. Integrating a small rapidly growing company into a larger, more established firm presented some serious roadblocks, but collaboratively my team worked through them and scaled to a bigger and better talent acquisition unit. On top of all the things I had already learned, I was now learning how companies operate and expand globally, which gave me exposure to big picture ideation and problem solving. As I continued to take on more responsibility and provide value in my role, I was promoted a couple of times and ultimately landed the role I have today. I'm fortunate to manage a team of 6 amazingly bright individuals and serve as the talent operations lead over all of North America. Who would have known that my small step backwards to get into a technology company, would lead to so much personal career growth!

My story is unique to my personal journey, but it is a real-life example of how the tactics and methods I suggest in this book can be applied to your job search. For anyone who feels lost when it comes to job seeking, I hope both my story and my perspective as a recruiter helps. While my experience certainly doesn't cover everything, understanding a bit about what is happening behind closed doors, can help guide your decisions and make your job search more comfortable, and fruitful!

Chapter 2

Identify your Priorities

One of the first steps in finding the right job is defining what "right" means for you. There are many factors that can contribute to your happiness in a role. The pandemic changed the game for employees and employers. Mental health, employee well-being, employee retention, candidate experience, inclusive culture, work-life balance, digital transformation, innovation - you've probably heard all these keywords buzzing around the past couple of years, and for good reason! It's crucial to identify what your priorities are for employment, so you can take a strategic approach to finding the best path for you at this stage of your life. Keep in mind that your priorities may change during the course of your career, as you are exposed to different companies, job functions, teams, and environments.

Remember my story in Chapter 1? My priorities changed a few times across my career. Each time I jumped back into a job search, it wasn't just a shot in the dark. I considered was passionate about, what was happening in the world, and what was most important to me at that specific point in my life, which ultimately led me in the right direction. Not quite sure what your own priorities are? Below are some definitions and context around things you will want to consider. While this isn't a complete list, these six core elements are common themes for many job seekers. Kick off your search by reviewing this list and rank each in order of importance. Later, I'll explain how you can use your prioritized list to find the best jobs for you.

- Compensation

- Culture

- Work Location

- Company Type and/or Industry

- Job Functions

- Growth and Career Advancement

COMPENSATION PACKAGE

Notice I include the word "package". Yes, this means money, but more importantly, the total package that an employer can offer you. Loosely defined, compensation is the monetary payment given to an individual in exchange for their services. This includes salary, hourly wages, commission and/or bonuses. In addition to monetary payment, some comp packages include benefits, stock options or equity, paid time off, 401K or other investment options for retirement, paid leaves for major life events, equipment, and other perks and incentives like discounts on cell phone bills, gym reimbursement, tuition reimbursement, etc. While some of the other items in a comp package don't directly translate to cash in your bank account, they can and will 100% affect your total out of pocket costs for the year and future years.

Think about the cost of living in your current city, your bills, your expenses, and the kind of lifestyle that you'd like to maintain. Do you prefer a steady stream of income evenly dispersed throughout the year? What are your spending habits? Would an end of year bonus help or hurt your cash flow? Consider what kind of health plans would be best for you and your family and/or dependents. Have you considered long term investments like 401K? What kind of employer contribution can help you reach those investment goals? What about time off for vacations, sick days, short term leaves, parental leaves? What do you see yourself doing this year? In the next couple of years? Do you pay for any courses or continued education on your own? Is equity important for your long-term goals?

These questions are meant to make you think. In all my years of recruiting, I've heard just about everything when I ask candidates what kind of compensation package they're looking for. Sometimes PTO takes trump, for folks who want flexibility to take vacations, spend more time with family, or simply step away for some mental solitude when they need it. For others, high-coverage health benefits for themselves and their families significantly annual out of pocket costs. Some people just flat out want to make as much money as possible, and that's OK too! It's your life and with the right contemplation and research, you'll soon identify what is most important in a compensation package.

COMPANY CULTURE

We're all familiar with this word, and we all use it, and many people list it as their number one priority for their job search. But how do we define it? If you Google company culture, you'll find many descriptions. I've included a few that I came across below:

- "How you do what you do in the workplace. It's the sum of your formal and informal systems and behaviors and values, all of which create an experience for your employees and customers."

- "The attitudes and behaviors of a company and its employees. It is evident in the way an organization's people interact with each other, the values they hold, and the decisions they make."

- "A shared set of values, goals, attitudes and practices that make up an organization."

- "How a company treats its employees and what they can expect from a life in that workplace."

Even though they're all different, you'll notice a few common keywords and themes. Culture is all about the core values of an organization, how they treat and interact with their employees, and how those values drive business decisions and organizational development.

Company culture preferences are different for everyone. I think we'd all agree we want a company that cares about its employees and demonstrates that. But what makes a company right for you? Let's start with a baseline view of culture. A lot of people associate culture with dress code. In ways dress code can connect to a company's core values. For example, if a company directly translates professionalism as business formal or business casual attire, it's likely that they'll require that attire for the office, or when meeting with clients, or for video meetings if you work remotely. This usually means no jeans, no flip flops, no t-shirts, no shorts. Some formal dress codes require ties or suits as well. Now consider a company that embodies innovation, creativity, or natural human interaction. They might have a more relaxed dress code, that empowers employees to wear whatever they would normally wear at home, or casually in public. There is certainly a spectrum and you'll come across companies in between, but ask yourself some questions to determine what parts of that spectrum you're open to. Do you prefer a relaxed environment where you can wear a t-shirt every day and grab beers with your coworkers? Or is type-A professionalism and business acumen more your thing?

There are of course several other values of an organization that contribute to its culture. Ask yourself the following questions: What kind of communication style do you find most effective? Do you like to joke around and build relationships with your coworkers and leaders? Or do you prefer business not to be mixed with pleasure? How much clarity do you need when it comes to job functions, career growth, and advancement? Can you deal with chaos, or do you prefer structure and order? How about a company's commitment to diversity, equity, and inclusion? Do you have concerns around feeling accepted or included? Have you ever experienced a lack of diversity and inclusion in a workplace? What kind of leadership style do you appreciate? What expectations do you have for leadership to provide transparency to the employee base? Do you cringe at the thought of micromanagement, or do you prefer hands-on direction? Do you enjoy collaborating with other people, or do you prefer to work alone, heads-down, totally focused?

You're going to read and research a lot about company culture as you go through your job search. Check out company social media pages, events, reviews, and ask around in your network as well. Pay attention to the things that excite you, or make you feel warm and fuzzy about working there. The way culture is described, will give you insight on how the company communicates with its employees, and if it's the type of environment that you'll thrive in. These are gut instincts that will help you gravitate towards the type of culture that you'll enjoy most.

WORK LOCATION

This one is pretty straightforward. Work location refers to the physical place that you will perform your role. Some people love working in an office. Usually these people really enjoy collaboration, face-to-face interaction, and separating their work life from their home life. Other reasons for working in an office might be to enjoy a high-rise view of an amazing city, or an endless list of superb lunch options right around the corner. If you like working in an office, you'll want to think about your commute, parking costs if applicable, and office hours. You may also consider relocating to a new city for the right job opportunity. Do your research on that market if you haven't lived there before, to be sure you'll enjoy the transition.

Another option for work location is a hybrid work schedule. This means that you work some days of the week in an office, and some days from home. Some people love this option because you get the best of both worlds. If an employer lists "hybrid" for their work location, make sure you understand the expectations exactly before committing to the role. You may find some companies that require a specific number of days onsite, while others only require onsite meetings.

Last but certainly not least...remote. I'd say this is a pretty popular option right now and quite common in many areas of the world, especially due to the pandemic. When you work remotely, you work from home, or from a coffee shop, or your personal rented office space - you choose where you will be most productive. Many people love working from home for the comfort, ability to eat/cook their own food, do laundry during the day, run to the gym during a lunch break, pick up kids from school at any time, etc.

Keep in mind that working from home doesn't necessarily mean you can work remotely from anywhere in the world. I can tell you firsthand as a talent acquisition professional, there are policies in place in every company that dictate where employees can legally be hired and work from home. Companies have specific jurisdictions in which they're set up to hire. This means your permanent residence needs to be in specific cities, states, regions, provinces and/or countries. In later chapters, I'll explain ways in which recruiters and/or postings themselves reveal remote working policies.

COMPANY TYPE AND/OR INDUSTRY

For those new to the professional career world, this can be one of the most confusing parts of job seeking! For experienced, tenured professionals, you may be considering a different type of environment that you haven't worked in before. Or perhaps you've seen it all, and you know exactly what kind of company best suits you. Either way, understanding the differences can help give you an idea of the pace, culture, or work-life balance you may experience depending on the type of company you work for.

- Corporate: Corporations can be small-medium sized or large, or very large. They're typically well-structured with defined career paths, processes, documentation, etc. If you have an A-type personality and you appreciate clear hierarchy and organizational structure, this could be the route for you. This is a good environment for people who crave strong direction, training, and well-established communication from the organization. You'll likely enter a role where the responsibilities are well-defined, which you'll be measured against for performance. And when you're ready to take the next step up in your career, you'll have a clear view of responsibilities and qualifications of other roles, how to move into them, and in some cases the timeline required to be promoted. This structure helps remove uncertainty around whether you're performing well, and when and how you can expect to grow in your career. Large corporations also tend to have competitive pay in comparison to national averages. Keep in mind, larger corporations still come with their fair share of surprises. Many job seekers want to work for the big-name brands or companies that everyone knows, but corporations tend to focus heavily on the bottom line and health of the company. You could experience bureaucracy and company politics, or surprise layoffs. Now don't get me wrong, not all corporations have negative qualities. There are many large organizations who care deeply for employees, prioritize culture and employee satisfaction, provide excellent benefits, pay, PTO, etc. We'll dive into this a bit more in chapters 2 and 3, so you know how to do your research on a company to see if it's right for you!

- Startups or privately owned companies: Startups or very small, privately owned companies certainly come with both pros and cons. There is usually a very close-knit, family style culture with a strong sense of community. A relaxed, casual dress code is common. Depending on your role, you may have the opportunity to impact the growth of the business in a huge way, which can be very exciting and rewarding. You may also see high compensation and other perks like RSU (restricted stock units). When/if a startup goes public or sells to a publicly traded company, you'll own that equity if your RSUs are fully vested. Depending on the value of the business when it's purchased or when it enters the public market, you could be walking into a pretty good financial situation. Startups and small companies typically have very fast-paced environments, and a general lack of structure as they scale. This isn't necessarily a bad thing, as long as you're comfortable embracing chaos and can thrive in an ambiguous environment. Unlike structured corporations, you shouldn't expect a lot of clarity around roles and responsibilities, or clear paths to career growth and promotions. For those who tend to take initiative on their own or enjoy taking on tasks that don't necessarily fall under their scope of work, this can be a really attractive environment.

- Agencies or Consulting Firms: An agency or consulting environment is common in fields like advertising, IT, software development, media, PR, marketing, financial services, mergers and acquisitions (M&A) and others. Typically, agencies make their revenue by providing services or solutions to other companies as a third-party partner. This means that they take on client project work, responsible for the planning and delivery of that work for a set price. Pricing models vary depending on the firm you work for. Some of these include retainers, staff augmentation, or managed services and statements of work. When you work at an agency, you often see a variety of different types of projects and challenges, and you'll get a taste for different verticals and industries as well. You may also interact with clients and/or stakeholders who are not part of your organization. So, if you're a people person, or interested in building communication skills, this could be an exciting environment! As far as pace and structure goes, agencies and consulting firms usually fall somewhere between large corporations and startups. When you're part of a services-driven organization, the pace of work will ebb and flow depending on client demand. While the baseline organizational structure is there, you'll likely find yourself taking on some hybrid and dynamic responsibilities to flex to the needs of the clients.

- Industries or Verticals: A company's primary industry or vertical can sometimes be its own category or a subcategory of company type. For example, if you've worked heavily in financial services, you might be open to a corporation, or a startup, or an agency, as long as it's in the financial services industry. Some companies operate in hybrid industries such as HealthTech, or healthcare technology, which would still be related to health or healthcare, but also blend with innovative software or wearables that track consumer health data. And wearable products might cross into the retail/consumer goods industry as well. Agencies and consulting firms either specialize in specific verticals, or work with clients across a different verticals. So those might be good company types to look out for if you're interested in learning about different industries! Keep in mind it's not always easy to switch from one vertical to another. It really depends on the company and how much they value industry subject matter expertise. I personally experienced this challenge when I attempted to move from creative recruiting to IT recruiting. However, by using an industry or vertical as a priority, you'll have a more targeted job hunt. A lot of organizations highlight their industry or vertical in effort to position themselves as "specialized" or experts in a niche.

Note: While these company types are quite prevalent within the "professional" job world, there are certainly other types of organizations out there that may be of interest to you. Some of these include government/federal entities, academia, and nonprofits and associations. I'm certainly not suggesting that these industries are not "professional". However, they may involve a slightly different process for job seekers regarding interviews, requirements, etc. The information provided in this job seeking guide can be more widely applied to the company types listed above.

JOB FUNCTIONS

Job functions refer to the tasks you'll be responsible for in your role on a day-to-day basis. A lot of people gloss over this part of their job search by focusing on job titles, company type and size, and compensation. But if you truly want to find a job that you enjoy, understanding the job functions is key. Think about the tasks or work activities that you really enjoy, the ones that you find energizing and exciting. On the flip side, think about the tasks or functions that you find less energizing, boring, or irritating. There will always be some small part of a role that you dislike. But if you see a lot of the functions you enjoy when reading through the responsibilities section of a job posting, it's probably a good match.

I suggest making a list of everything you've done in previous roles. What did your day-to-day look like? What about other tasks or functions you were responsible for in some other cadence? How much of your role was spent doing each of those tasks? Were there too many tasks? Would you have preferred to focus on a few specific areas and drop the others if it was up to you? By reflecting on past experiences, or even reflecting on schoolwork if you're new to the job world, you'll gain an understanding of what motivates you on a daily basis, and what things you'll get sick of. For some people, job functions are most important, because it doesn't matter where they work or who they work with, if they're doing a job that they love and find fulfilling. Personally, I think job functions hold a lot of weight, as long as they're paired with the right combination of my other job preferences. I've also talked about job hunting with some close friends, who just aren't as career-motivated as they used to be. They prefer a cushy role with limited challenges to get through the day and take home a paycheck. Now, I haven't had any candidates blatantly say this to me in an interview, but I'm sure there are others who quietly share this same perspective. There's nothing wrong with either route by the way. Just be honest with yourself so you know how to properly rank job functions on your list of priorities.

GROWTH AND CAREER ADVANCEMENT

Even though you're looking for a specific job right now, it's important to think about your long game. Not 100% sure what path you want to go down? That's OK too! Part of finding the right career is trying different roles and tasks, finding your groove, and learning what suits you best. However, you don't want to get stuck in a company where you have zero growth or upward mobility. Growth and career advancement refers to the structure that a company has in place for employees to move within their respective career paths. This could mean taking on more responsibilities, receiving a promotion or compensation increase, changes to your title, leading or managing others, etc. Do you see yourself managing direct reports, or leading or mentoring a team? Do you prefer to perform as an individual contributor and improve your skills without the responsibilities of coaching and mentoring others? Do you get bored easily with doing repetitive job functions for extended periods of time? What kinds of career transitions have you seen others make, who are in the role that you do now? Do you like to start with a new and fresh challenge every couple of years?

When looking at job descriptions and company websites or social media pages, pay attention to whether they mention career advancement and growth. Organizations who support their employees with personal career goals and passions tend to talk about it publicly. Some companies offer opportunities for continued education, training, or mentorship programs, which allow you to keep developing new skills. If that's something that is important to you, you might already be taking the initiative to do continuous learning on your own. However, having a company who supports that, or provides the resources or reimburses you for completing that continued learning is even better!

Ok, you have your list of priorities, and you're ready to dive in and start looking at jobs, now what? Well, it depends on what you've listed as your top priorities. In the next two chapters we'll look at which job seeking method suits you best, based on your priority ranking. If company type, company culture, or growth and career advancement trend towards the top of your list, you might want to start with a "company-first" method (Chapter 3). This involves researching the companies you'd like to work for first, followed by reviewing positions they have available. If compensation, work location or job functions hold more weight, the "job-first" method (Chapter 4) recommends starting with open roles or live postings, and diving into the company details afterwards. If you prefer to take a back seat approach and set yourself up for recruiters to come to you, you'll enjoy the "reactive method" (Chapter 5).

Chapter 3

Company-First Job Seeking

Company-first job seekers will find a lot of value by investing time upfront on research, rather than diving right into job boards. A great place to start is LinkedIn. While most job boards and aggregators offer a small blurb or section about the company within their job description, LinkedIn offers full company profiles that give you much more information about the organization. On a company's LinkedIn page, you'll find "about us", the industry or vertical, company type, number of employees, who works there now, where those employees are located, what the company does, how long they've been in business, their official website, and links to external social media pages as well. Digital presence is more important now than ever. So, the information portrayed on these pages, as well as job descriptions, should provide a pretty accurate representation of the company. In most cases, the content and verbiage shown is a collaboration of insights from talent acquisition, leaders, hiring managers, marketing, and HR.

If you're not sure where to begin on LinkedIn, try some Googling first. Research articles online such as "best companies to work for", "top companies for [blank] industry", "fastest growing companies in [location]", etc. You can search for whatever makes sense for you. If you recall from my personal story, I used the company first method when I wanted to get out of advertising but still work in something peripheral enough for it to make sense as a transition. I tried searching things like "what industries you can transition into after advertising". I used this method again when I decided on technology and IT services as my target. I searched for those keywords in my specific location and found a bunch of companies that I had never heard of. I started by searching those company profiles on LinkedIn and reviewed their careers pages. Even though some of them didn't have openings for recruiters, I messaged HR and recruiting teams on LinkedIn and ended up kickstarting a conversation, simply because I had shown interest in the organization. As you're reviewing your own search results, you can follow the same process. Check out the company pages on LinkedIn to find out what industry they're in, what type of organization they are, how many people work there, and how long they've been around. Look at their website and social pages to learn about culture and career advancement, social activities, and employee engagement.

Glassdoor is another awesome place to check out company profiles. It's well known for providing transparency around compensation ranges at each company, as well as reviews on working for the company, from either past or current employees. Glassdoor company profiles also offer insight into their interview process, provided by previous interviewees, even if that individual didn't end up working there. Checking out a company's overall rating on Glassdoor can give you an idea of whether people enjoy working there and why. You can find a ton of great content from real people who have direct experience either interviewing with or working for that organization.

THE ACTION PLAN

Next, create a list of 30-40 companies that look interesting and fit your main criteria, after reviewing them online. Remember, your focus is the company itself. Ensure these companies are within the industry or company type you're open to, align with the culture you desire, and show some indication of your preferred career growth and advancement options. Once you've established a list, check out both the careers page on their website, as well as their open roles listed on LinkedIn or other job boards. Try searching for some of the titles or job functions you're seeking first. If you don't see an open role at the company that aligns perfectly, it may be worthwhile to apply to something close. You might be able to get your foot in the door and speak with their recruiting team to learn more about other roles. If there's absolutely nothing in the realm of the job you're seeking, try looking at existing employees on LinkedIn to see if anyone performs that kind of job currently.

Many organizations have a "general interest in employment / career opportunities" email address or "contact us" form. If a particular company really strikes your interest, try sending your resume to those generic mailboxes, with some indication of the type of role you're seeking, and why that company stood out to you. Talent acquisition forecasting is always going on behind the scenes, but not all roles may be posted live at the time of your job search. It doesn't hurt to get your information in the company system, just in case there is a new posting coming soon that hasn't hit the job boards yet. Sometimes having an initial conversation with someone from recruiting or HR can open doors as well. Remember that talent acquisition professionals are tasked with helping to scale and grow organizations with talented people who will provide value. A great conversation can lead to a new opportunity, even if there's not an exact role available that matches your background.

Also, consider using your network of connections on LinkedIn, see if you know anyone who already works there, and ask for an introduction to the recruiting team or the hiring manager. A 2021 Forbes article about job seeking shares *"Getting in front of decision-makers is the hardest part of the job search because it feels like it's completely out of your control."* Be bold and take control! Try different routes, utilize your powerful network, shoot your shot even if it's a long shot. Feeling extra ambitious? You can also look up current employees who are in similar roles to one that you're looking for. Reach out to them to ask them why they enjoy working there. You'd be surprised at how transparent a stranger will be. Now don't expect an answer from everyone, especially if you don't know them personally. But some will be more than happy to shed some light on the company, their role, or even the culture. And who knows, perhaps that might be your way in if that individual knows of an upcoming vacancy on their team.

Information about culture and career growth and advancement is probably the most challenging to acquire online. By using some of the suggestions above like reviewing websites and social channels, you will get some perspective. However, actually knowing someone or speaking to someone candidly about the company will give you a more grounded view. Admittedly, companies aren't going to be 100% transparent about their flaws or organizational challenges on their digital channels. If you're unable to connect with anyone within the company itself, my suggestion earlier about Glassdoor is a close second. At least you know these are real people who have worked in that company and can provide their personal experience and perspective. Pay attention to the dates on reviews though, companies change over time and the culture and opportunities may be different now than they were 2-3 years ago.

Benefits of This Method

Let's talk a bit about why and how this method can improve your job search. First and foremost, you're doing research upfront about the company before you apply. Sometimes when you apply blindly to roles, and then begin interviewing, you quickly realize the industry, or company size, or even the culture is not really what you're looking for. This can happen within the very first conversation with a Recruiter, or in subsequent interviews. Have you ever applied to a job, received a request for an interview, and then looked at the company website to refresh your memory? Did that make you more excited or less excited about the interview?

Personally, I've experienced both situations, but in some cases felt a bit of regret for applying because once I took a second look, I knew the company wouldn't be right for me. I wished I would have spent more time researching the company before deciding to apply and committing to an interview. It's tough when you're eager for a new job. You tend to throw your hat in the ring for a lot of things. But at the end of the day, your interview conversations could unfold some major discrepancies between what you want, and what that company has to offer. You don't want to waste time and energy applying to and interviewing at companies you are not truly excited about. Instead, channel that time and energy into pre-application research, so there's a higher likelihood that the position will end up being a realistic career choice. Excitement about a company naturally shines during the interview process. Recruiters can sense when candidates don't seem all that interested in the work the company does, or the industry that they're in. Recruiters also tend to capture written feedback following a phone conversation. When hiring managers read through interview feedback, those small details can be a deciding factor on whether to move forward with the next interview.

When your established list of companies stems from conducting your own research, you'll take comfort in knowing that any interview requests you receive will be something you're excited about exploring. And if the available job itself doesn't quite line up, so be it. But you've now made a connection at a company that you feel good about, and you're willing to explore job opportunities there, whether now or in the future.

One tip for company-first job seekers: when possible, try to seek out and research companies that are at least loosely aligned to your background. Yes, company-first job seeking is truly about finding organizations that fit your most precious criteria. However, if there's a complete disconnect between your experience and the organizations you're applying to, there's a good chance you won't stand out among other applicants. Let's say you have a history of working in healthcare, but you're super interested in getting into marketing. You can start by researching marketing firms or marketing technology companies who service healthcare clients. While you may not have marketing experience, you have industry knowledge and connections in healthcare. If a recruiter reviews 10 resumes of marketing professionals with zero healthcare experience, and then sees yours, your industry background might be just the right criteria to land you an interview.

If there's no obvious connection like relevant industry experience, you can also try to align your social profiles and resume to the industries and/or companies you're seeking to join. Recruiters are going to review your resume, your LinkedIn profile, and sometimes other social media profiles as well. Maybe you've worked in nonprofits your entire career, because you deeply care about causes like environmental sustainability, or medical research, or support for veterans, etc. When you're researching companies, see if any of them talk about their commitment to these causes, if they're contributing or donating, doing pro-bono work to support them, or offering employees paid volunteer time. If a company is very vocal about social responsibility, it's likely that the company values and internal culture will align with yours. Highlight your involvement on your resume, and follow related pages on LinkedIn, or join social media groups with active discussions or events related to the causes you are passionate about. This visibility to your interests, involvement, and passions, can also help set you apart from other candidates. Recruiting is all about finding the right set of both hard skills and soft skills for each and every hire. It really depends on how hiring managers and organizations prioritize their qualifications. Again, job seeking/hiring is a two-way street, so if you're excited about the company's values, and they see that you hold those same values, you're more likely to land an interview.

When I worked in staffing, I saw this technique prove successful time and time again for early talent, aka fresh graduates. We had several advertising agencies as clients, and when they were looking for junior staff, passion projects and interests trumped internship experience. New graduate candidates were more likely to get interviews if they made "mock" ad campaigns for some of their favorite brands and added them to their portfolios. And if they followed major ad agencies or advertising holding companies on LinkedIn, it was considered a plus to the hiring managers. This was largely due to the values and culture of most advertising agencies. They're all about big picture ideas, conceptual thinking, and fresh and inventive perspectives. Some of the junior candidates had 3-month internships as graphic designers under their belt, which gave them real world experience with hard skills, such as technical proficiency with design tools like Photoshop, InDesign, and Illustrator. They had the right building blocks, but their passion and mindset didn't click as well with hiring managers, in comparison to candidates with no experience yet more passion for advertising.

Sharing the previous example about recent graduates brings up another interesting item to consider. Your passions, interests, and sometimes even values may change over time. As you advance in your career, you're going to learn a lot about the work you enjoy, the type of people you prefer to work with, and the expectations you have for an employer of choice. Let's pretend you land your dream job right out of school, and you fall in love with the position and the company. The job is life. You're eager to advance in your career, you're working super hard, contributing immense value, and being rewarded handsomely along the way. Four years in, your personal life takes a turn. Maybe you decide to have kids and want to take more time than a standard parental leave. Or you or your partner encounter a serious medical issue, and you need to step away for an extended period of time. You assume your hard work and tenure has proven invaluable to the company, and you go to a manager to discuss the situation openly and weigh your options. Suddenly, the tables turn, and you realize the company policies have very poor support for this kind of situation. Your manager and other leaders make little effort to compromise and now you must make a choice to stay or go. You can already feel the company plotting to backfill your position as soon as possible. The work needs to be performed, regardless of who's doing it, and without considering the time and effort you've contributed in the past. OK, to be fair this is an extreme example, and I hope this never happens to you! But the takeaway is that sometimes your priorities are shaped by bad experiences. At times it's easier to define what you don't want, versus what you do want. Following this kind of scenario, you might prioritize researching companies with strong employee reviews, social profiles that boast best places to work or employee satisfaction scores, or benefits that highlight unique policies beyond the standard PTO and retirement options.

I recently learned the career history of one of the senior leaders at my company. For the purposes of this example, I'll use the alias Jared. Jared spent 10 years working at large financial services organizations, and he had a very clear growth path ahead of him. He knew he would continue to move upward in his career, and the path to financial stability and retirement was laid out for him and his family. One of his colleagues left the bank and started his own company. While the colleague tried to pursue Jared to join, he was comfortable and stable, and a career move was too risky. Jared began to feel a bit frustrated with the large corporate environment - the pace, the politics, and the resistance to change and innovate. He knew joining a startup wouldn't be as stable as his current role, but he also knew he no longer felt passionate about the organization he was at. After about a year of contemplation, he took that risk and joined his colleagues' startup. Jared was a bit out of his element, as he was used to well-defined structure and process. But over time, he was able to utilize his knowledge, experience, strategy, and passion to help expand the startup into an established firm. Jared excelled in this environment, and quickly realized his innovative ideas and entrepreneurial spirit had been stifled at his previous employer. After 7-8 years of expansion and success, this startup became part of a large, rapidly growing global services firm. He now serves as a leader in many areas such as marketing, sales, brand awareness, and organizational improvements on an enterprise level. I share this anecdote to further support the idea that sometimes your career choices are shaped by experiences that weren't really the right fit for you in the first place. Pay attention to those gut feelings, they'll help steer you in the right direction!

Chapter 4

Job-First Method

Job-first job seekers can start their search on popular job boards and job aggregators. I mentioned these in the previous chapter, and I'm sure you've heard of them before, but what is the difference? Job boards tend to have a specialty like niche industry or type of positions, and companies pay to post their positions on those specialty boards. Job aggregators scrape the web for thousands of jobs and pull them into one place, so job seekers can search through expansive lists of positions that fall into their scope.

Some job boards and aggregators are free for both employers and job seekers, others follow a paid membership model, or paid job posting model. If you are looking for volume, job aggregators are a good option. They will have thousands of jobs listed from other websites and job boards. The downside is you'll probably spend a lot of time sifting through pages and pages of jobs to find ones that you actually like. Filtering functionality varies between different platforms, so I'd suggest trying a few and seeing which ones produce the best results for you. Niche job boards are great if you want a shorter, more tailored list of jobs that align to your skills and job priorities.

Here's a list of some of the most used, most popular job aggregator search engines in the US, that have a high number of postings:

- LinkedIn
- Indeed
- Monster
- Google Jobs
- CareerBuilder
- ZipRecruiter

Here are some examples of niche job boards that are tailored to specific criteria:

- Dice - IT or technical positions
- Ladders - high paying positions, typically 100K or higher in annual salary
- Clearance Jobs - positions for applicants who have government security clearance, typically for the defense industry
- FlexJobs - remote and flexible positions around the world
- College Recruiter and Handshake - entry level or junior positions for college graduates or early career professionals
- Coroflot and Dribbble - creative and design positions, where you can also host your own portfolio
- AngelList - positions with early-stage startups

- Sales Heads and Rainmakers - sales and business development positions

Note: There are thousands of niche job boards out there. Some will be more effective than others, but if you're looking for something specific, it's worth doing some research. Try to look for niche boards that offer at least 100 or more positions. If the job board has less, it's likely that it's not established enough to draw in a good variety of employers.

REVIEWING JOB POSTINGS

Start on each job platform by searching for the title of the job you're looking for. You can also put the title in as a keyword to find anything relatable. As you read through results, you may find other titles that list similar job functions and responsibilities. Consider incorporating those titles into your search as well. Titles are different at every company, and you might not be familiar with every title you see. If the responsibilities and requirements align to what you're looking for, those unfamiliar titles could help expand your options.

Here's an example. You're in sales and you're looking for a sales role. You begin searching job platforms with the word "sales" as a keyword. You get a huge range of job title results such as Sales Manager / Director, Business Development Manager, Lead Generation Executive, Business Development Representative, Account Executive, Account Manager, Customer Success Manager, Sales Trainer, Sales Manager, etc. Not all these roles are going to be exactly what you're looking for, but reading the descriptions will help you identify if the role itself lines up with your experience. If you want to trim down your list, reading descriptions across multiple titles will help identify trends of job responsibilities that are usually associated with each title. Moving forward, you can narrow your search to those titles, so you have a higher likelihood of finding the right match.

A word of caution though, just because certain titles tend to align with a specific set of skills or responsibilities, doesn't mean that will always be the case. Why is this so confusing? Well, within each company there are naming conventions used to maintain organizational structure, and expectations for each role. Some recruiting teams post positions with a unique company-specific title, while others will change it to reflect typical titles that exist on the market. It's the same position either way, but considering TA teams all approach job postings differently, casting a wider net isn't a bad idea. You can also do some research online for typical titles that fall under the type of job functions you're looking for.

A few years back, I was tasked with finding and hiring a Scrum Master. Scrum is an agile project management framework that helps teams structure and manage their work through a set of values, principles, and practices. It's commonly used in the IT world, but it can be applied to many types of organizations. The title Scrum Master has become widely adopted and aligns to roles that require specific experience and training versus a general Project Manager role. Our company had a specific naming convention for titles within our Project Management unit, and the role itself was called "Project Manager", even though we wanted Scrum experience. Since I knew we needed the skills of a Scrum Master, the hiring manager and I decided our public posting should read "Scrum Master".

I began searching for candidates and set up some interviews with folks who had the background and experience we were seeking. One interviewee in particular was phenomenal. Not only did he have all the right qualifications, but his communication was excellent, and he had the ability to lead teams and interact with clients. After a couple of conversations, the interview process led into a demo project which was completed by all candidates for this business unit. The demo project read "Project Manager Demo Project" because of the naming convention that we had internally. I got an abrupt email from the candidate saying he was no longer interested. I was so confused, as he seemed super engaged throughout the process so far! So I gave him a call to find out what was going on. He disclosed that he was looking for a Scrum Master role, and after seeing that demo project he assumed we were looking for a project manager and named our position improperly. I took some time to explain the internal structure and naming conventions, and also reiterated the responsibilities of the role, which were in fact very aligned to a Scrum Master position. He felt a bit more comfortable after that call and agreed to continue the interview process. I also shared his concerns with the hiring manager as she would be part of the final interview. After completing the interview process and learning more about the organization and role, he felt totally comfortable moving forward, and accepted an offer to join our team!

For the record, he's still employed at this company now and is thriving in his role as a Scrum Master. He was so close to walking away from an opportunity simply because the title didn't 100% match what he was looking for. When reviewing jobs, the responsibilities and requirements will paint a much better picture of the actual job than the title will. This can go in the opposite direction as well. If you're set on a particular title, make sure you read the details before applying. Sometimes titles are not truly matched with what the job entails.

The takeaway here is to read everything in the job description regardless of the title. And if and when you have the opportunity to interview, ask questions to make sure the title and the role are what you expected. If you simply apply to any and every posting that has the "right title", you're probably going to waste time interviewing for a job you won't want. This is something I've heard frequently from marketing candidates. There are a ton of marketing positions posted every day that are actually sales roles. This is partially due to crossover - marketing and sales teams work in tandem when the goal of marketing is to drive new business and brand awareness for potential customers. You may think you're applying to a marketing role because the word marketing is in the title. But if you read the description thoroughly, you might see job functions that are more typically aligned to sales, such as generating leads, prospecting, pitching the company to customers, etc. If compensation or pay ranges are visible, that can be another indicator. Sales roles usually have some kind of commission model, where a corporate marketing job is likely to be salaried or hourly.

RESEARCH ADDITIONAL INFORMATION

Now that we've covered job functions, let's think about some other priorities that are important when using the "job-first" method, such as the compensation package. Most listings include a brief description of the company, the main job responsibilities, required skills and experience, preferred skills, and high-level overview of their benefits. Some companies list compensation in their descriptions, and some don't. So, you might not learn this information until the first interview with a recruiter. Pay transparency is not consistently required for job postings across all regions or countries in the world...yet. In the US specifically, there are already several states that require job posting pay transparency by law, and many other states are likely to follow suit.

Pay transparency is a very hot topic right now and we're trending towards more robust pay transparency laws in the near future. This can be extremely helpful for disqualifying jobs that aren't going to meet your basic compensation requirements. Business Insider is an awesome source of truth for existing pay transparency laws and laws that are going into effect soon. You'll see a breakdown for each state or region, and understand what employers are required to share with you and when. Many locations have laws where compensation range is only required to be disclosed if/when a candidate asks for it. So if you live in one of those regions, ask! When you know your rights based on your location, it helps remove some of the awkwardness of compensation convos with recruiters.

Job location, another standard priority of the job-first method, is a hot topic right now as well. During the peak of the pandemic nearly everyone was working remotely. Thousands of companies adopted a permanently remote working environment and did not require employees to work in physical office locations. Recently, many companies changed back to onsite or hybrid, requiring staff to work part time or full time in physical office locations. If you enjoy working remotely and only want to consider remote positions, you'll want to check for that on job postings. Most job sites, like LinkedIn for example, allow you to filter your results for remote-only positions, which will help narrow your list. Read any verbiage about location carefully and ask about it when you connect with talent acquisition. Working from home may only apply if you live in a certain state, or it could be a remote role that involves some travel to office or client locations. If you're open to hybrid or onsite roles, it might be worth your while to target these positions first. Quite frankly a lot of companies are losing employees who have grown accustomed to working from home, by requiring them to come back into the office. In the past year or so, I have interviewed countless job seekers who claim the only reason they're searching for a new position is due to a company requirement to work in the office again. Onsite or hybrid roles may have a lower number of applicants, or possibly smaller "pipeline" of candidates due to the location requirements of the role. If that's a major checkpoint on the recruiter's list of must haves, you'd already have a leg up against the competition.

As you are evaluating positions and determining which ones you want to apply for, there are a few additional things to consider. I'll cover these more in depth in the "Applications" chapter of this book, but here's a quick preview. When applying, it's ideal to apply on the company website directly. This ensures your resume and information reaches the correct person internally, and that you provide everything they require to consider your candidacy. Another best practice for job seeking is to keep a running list of the companies and roles you've applied to. You might even consider ranking them in order of interest before you start applying. Knock out your top picks first and apply to the rest later if they're less desirable for you.

If you're using popular job boards or aggregators to find open positions, consider signing up for job alerts for similar roles. You'll see this technique explained further in the next chapter about reactive job seeking. You've already done some research upfront and identified the types of positions you want to target. These job platforms use algorithms to collect and share positions with similar titles and responsibilities, so it takes some of the work off your plate.

Remember that all these methods are anchored to the common goal of all recruiters: effective hiring. While the job-first method helps you target positions that you really want, there should still be some connection to your actual experience. In the previous chapter we talked about how industry experience, or passion and values can help you stand out, even if you don't have the exact "hard skills" for the role.

As a job-first seeker, you're using a job posting's listed qualifications, compensation, and/or job location as your checkpoint on whether to apply or not.

You might find a few postings that perfectly match your compensation and location, but if the job functions are way off from your experience, don't expect perfect harmony. Recruiters might not even reach out if you don't meet some of the basic qualifications or experience. After all, they are tasked with narrowing the application pool to the candidates who are most likely to be hired. If you do get the chance to interview, be prepared to answer tough questions and showcase your ability to adapt and learn a role that you haven't done before. You might be presented with a more extensive screening process than other candidates who are a more obvious match on paper. All that said, you could still absolutely come out as the front runner! But if you get the job, and you're extremely unfamiliar with the job you're tasked with, no doubt you'll have a few challenges ahead of you. This isn't a bad thing if you're open to challenges and comfortable with growing pains in a new role. It also depends quite a bit on the company and what kind of training and support they offer for new employees. Those would be good questions to ask a recruiter or hiring manager, as well as how success will be measured in the role.

As a rule of thumb, I highly recommend you target positions with qualifications and responsibilities that match at least 60% or more of your background. Why 60%? Well, there was an interesting gender-related statistic released by a Hewlett Packard study several years back. This statistic has been quoted frequently and rehashed by industry publications across the years. At the root of it, the study showed that men tend to apply for jobs that they're 60% qualified for, while women usually apply only when they're 100% qualified. The takeaway is that it is absolutely possible for anyone to be hired for a position where they don't meet all the requirements. You don't want to miss out on a great opportunity by assuming that you won't be considered! One quick way to evaluate this percentage is to go through the listed "qualifications" or "requirements" on the job listing one by one. Ask yourself if you meet that requirement - yes or no - and then tally up the yes's and divide those yes's by the total number of requirements listed. If it's 60% or higher, go for it.

BENEFITS OF THIS METHOD

Remember that when you're using the job-first method, you're prioritizing the position itself and the parameters that come with that role - meaning job functions, location, and compensation. Naturally, you're going to have some preferences in mind across the other priorities as well, including company type, culture, and organizational career growth and advancement. The purpose of ranking your priorities is to identify what matters most to you, so you can be a bit more flexible with lower-ranked priorities.

Let's say you always imagined yourself in a corporate setting, with clearly defined structure for advancement, and you feel your personality would fit better in a type-A business professional culture. During your job search, you come across an amazing job with all the right responsibilities, location, and compensation range with a small startup. You've already decided that putting the job first is more important to you, so perhaps a totally different environment isn't such a bad thing? When you focus on the things that will bring you joy and fulfillment in a role, I promise that some of the other factors won't matter as much when you step into the role. You might even realize that you love the startup environment and culture even more than a corporate setting after you get used to it. And that can help fuel your job search journey for future roles with other startups. While a startup might not have clearly defined growth paths when you join, that can certainly change over time, and might even work out to your advantage. That startup may grow at a rapid pace and double or triple in size within one or two years, and as the company grows, you'll grow as well. Or perhaps the startup will be acquired by a much larger, more established company. This might shift the culture and structure into more of a corporate setting, which is what you were originally hoping for!

As a reminder from my personal story in Chapter 1, I joined a small 150-person company because I was laser focused on my priorities: getting into the technology industry with a specific focus on services or consulting firms. I was leaving a huge organization with 35+ locations, but I took a leap of faith. I also originally applied for a management role, got shot down, and then reapplied to a mid-level individual contributor position, for which I was hired. Even though the second job wasn't as interesting as the first, I knew I had the right qualifications and was confident that I could be successful. Shortly after, my 150-person company turned into a global organization with 13,000 employees through means of acquisition. My opportunity for career growth exploded, due to the company's focus on expanding North America.

Less than two years after joining, I moved into a management role. Obviously, this can go both ways, not every story will have a happy ending. But I think it's important to follow your gut when considering which positions to apply to. Don't hesitate to compare each role against your top priorities, and determine whether it's worth flexing a bit on the others.

Chapter 5

Reactive Job Seeker Approach

Being a reactive job seeker doesn't mean you won't ever submit an application, but there are some ways to ensure that recruiters and hiring companies come to you, which makes the job seeking process easier! A few strategies include improving and updating your LinkedIn profile, creating a "must-have" list of qualifiers, signing up for automated job listing emails, and partnering with third parties who offer free recruiting services.

UPDATING YOUR LINKEDIN PROFILE

Improving and updating your LinkedIn profile is much more impactful than it sounds. LinkedIn is one of the most powerful tools used by talent acquisition teams to source and attract new talent. As of 2023, LinkedIn boasts 875 million users globally, with 75 million company profiles. The country with the most users is the United States, followed by China and India. [7] Because this platform is the largest social network for professionals, recruiters use it as a tool to proactively search for qualified candidates. This includes both active job seekers, and reactive, or passive candidates who are not actively applying. Let's talk about how LinkedIn works, and how employers and recruiters use it.

I'll preface this by sharing that there are different versions of products available to hiring teams. These include LinkedIn Recruiter, Recruiter Lite, Jobs, Talent Insights, Recruiter System Connect, and TalentHub (which is essentially an ATS tool). I share this because recruiters can only use certain functionality depending on the products their company pays for. But generally, most companies with established talent acquisition teams use LinkedIn Recruiter or LinkedIn Recruiter Lite, which have the most functionality for sourcing and researching candidate profiles. When recruiters look for candidates on LinkedIn, one method is writing custom boolean strings to produce a list of candidate profiles with their search criteria. Boolean strings are algorithms that use simple functions to include and exclude relevant keywords. The keywords can literally be anything, but most commonly include technologies, industries, verticals, job skills, certifications, education, company names, etc. By including specific keywords relevant to your experience on your profile, you'll show up in search results when recruiters are looking for those keywords.

There are also built in features within LinkedIn itself, which can be used as search filters by recruiting teams. While these aren't as customizable as boolean strings, the features are available to both recruiters and users. This means that all users can edit their profile, and choose to include keywords, preferences, skills, and experience relevant to each section. Below is a breakdown of each editable segment of your

LinkedIn Profile. The fields in bold can be used by recruiters as a filtering tool. We'll go through each of these fields, so you know where and how to edit them to get the most action as a reactive jobseeker.

Open To

Headline

Current Position

Industry

Education

Location/City

About

Experience

Skills

Recommendations (while this technically does not allow for filtering, it holds a lot of weight with recruiters, which I'll cover later)

"Open To" meaning "open to work", appears as a button directly under your profile picture and name. This button is a reactive job-seeker's best friend. Select that you're open to finding a new job and fill in your preferences. You can choose preferred job titles, locations (including remote, onsite or hybrid), start date or timing, and job type (full time, part time, contract, etc.). While recruiters may try to contact candidates who are passive and not looking for new jobs, the average response rate from candidates who are "open to work" is significantly higher. If you're looking for recruiters to come to you, be prepared because this will open the InMail floodgates. Adding preferences is a good way to weed out messages from recruiters with jobs that are not of interest to you. Personally, I read these preferences before contacting a candidate. I make sure the job I plan to share with them aligns with the titles they're looking for, their location, and their preferred employment type. If I have a mid-level position, and the candidate indicates they're looking for Director or VP titles, it doesn't make sense for me to reach out to them. And frankly, I might even offend them by asking.

The Headline field is a place to add your current or preferred job title, or a combination of keywords, titles, certifications, or skills that you want to highlight. This is an open text field with no character limit. You can add as much content as you like but remember that it appears right under your profile name, so you don't want a massive paragraph there. Think of it as a general objective that you'd put on a resume, or a short sentence that accurately captures your skillset. As a reactive job seeker, you'll want to include the job title or two that you are targeting, and maybe add an industry you've worked in. You could also sneak in a certification you've completed if it's relevant to the type of jobs you're looking for. When recruiters search for those specific keywords, your profile will appear in their results since they are listed in your headline. Here's an example for an IT professional who is looking for a Cloud Architecture role: "Cloud Architect. Microsoft Azure Certified. Financial Services Experience." A profile with this headline will appear to recruiters who are looking for "Cloud + Azure" or

"Architect + Financial Services" or "Azure + Financial Services", or similar combinations.

Current position is pretty straightforward, it's the title you currently hold at your place of employment. In the intro section of your profile, you will see this field, but it's actually a drop-down list of the positions populated from your experience section. You'll need to edit your experience section in order to select your current position from this drop-down. If your title is niche or specific to your company, edit this to a more commonly used title. For example, the company I work for now has an internal title called "Industry Consultant", but it's essentially a Product Owner role within a specific vertical. So instead of using the internal company title, a user could use "Product Owner" which would make their profile visible to recruiters who are looking for people with that title. Whenever possible, try to use the recommended list of titles that LinkedIn provides, rather than writing the exact word-for-word title that you hold. Those drop-down lists appear as filters for recruiters, so you're more likely to show up in recruiter searches when you use a recommended title from LinkedIn.

The industry field is also a drop-down list provided by LinkedIn. It's most commonly used by recruiters at companies who prefer candidates from a similar company, or a direct competitor. This field will be more relevant for some reactive job seekers than others. Companies in highly regulated industries like healthcare or finance typically look for previous industry experience, for other companies the industry won't matter much. Regardless, it's required by LinkedIn so you will have to select something.

Education is optional, so you can choose to include all, some, or none of your education if you wish. Some companies have specific education requirements for hiring, so it doesn't hurt to add yours to avoid getting contacted for a role where you don't meet that requirement. You can also list continued education courses from online schools or bootcamps, which can help you stand out to recruiters.

Location / City is primarily used by recruiters who can only hire candidates in specific locations or time zones. For example, if a company needs someone who lives in the Pacific Time Zone in the United States, they might filter LinkedIn to only show candidates in west coast states. If you're relocating to a new city, and you're looking for recruiters to contact you about positions in that area, I'd suggest putting that city as your location, rather than the city you live in now. You can add your relocation plans to your "about" section as well (see next paragraph) to help avoid confusion.

The about section is great place to load up your profile with relevant keywords and keyword strings that are directly related to your experience and strengths. Boolean searches performed by recruiters scrape the entire about section, to populate related candidate profiles into their search results. It's a free-range text box so you can include other context about what you're looking for. Perhaps a few phrases for recruiters to read pertaining to your personal top priorities. Consider listing the job titles or functions you're looking for, or what kinds of company values are important to you, or even the compensation range you're targeting. Remember that as a reactive job seeker, the more information you clarify upfront, the easier it will be for recruiters to find your profile and reach out with extremely relevant opportunities.

Within the experience section, try to treat this as much like a resume as possible. Make sure your job history is updated and correct and add some context for each role on the work or job functions you held there. I've often seen detailed descriptions of projects and/or initiatives that candidates performed during a past role. Think about sharing project details in a case study format - what was the problem, solution, and outcome? Not only will this aggregate your profile with additional keywords, but it will help recruiters understand the context and complexity of your role, versus guessing based on a title alone. Having only the name of the company, your title, and the dates of employment leaves a lot to be desired for recruiters. It's also a nice touch to add a short blurb about the company you worked for within each past experience. Recruiters often look for candidates who come from similar companies, industries, or competitors. Now they can certainly click on the company page and do a bit of research on their own, but giving some context upfront might prompt them to contact you more quickly than someone who doesn't have that information listed. The more robust your profile is, the more likely you will be to receive requests from recruiters.

Skills and Skills Assessments are by far some of a recruiter's most frequented sections. LinkedIn allows you to select skills that you are proficient in, and some even offer a skill evaluation. If completed, that skill will show as a "LinkedIn certified skill". This appears differently on the recruiter's dashboard, and recruiters can filter by certified skills as well. You can also ask your network to endorse you for skills. I find the best way to receive endorsements is to directly message some of your coworkers or past connections and ask them to endorse you. As a recruiter, if I'm looking for 3 top skills, and a candidate's profile has 10 or more endorsements for those exact 3 skills, I will reach out to them right away. Endorsements for skills give your profile an extra element of credibility or validity, in comparison to simply listing them yourself. On a positive note, whenever you add new connections, LinkedIn will automatically "suggest" your new connection to endorse you for the skills you have listed!

While recommendations are not something you can edit yourself, it is another excellent function of LinkedIn! Reach out to some previous coworkers and/or managers and ask them to write you a recommendation - you'd be surprised at how many colleagues are willing to help. LinkedIn makes it easy by providing a "request a recommendation" button where you can message a first connection and include some context as to why you're asking for the recommendation. You can also offer to write them a recommendation as well, so it's a fair trade off.

CREATING A QUALIFIER LIST

Creating a qualifier list for your ideal role is similar to the "pre-screening" process that recruiters use to narrow their candidate funnels. It should consist of a few must-have requirements that will allow you to rule out positions early on. This is a good way to reserve your precious interview time for quality roles. It can also drive recruiters away who may be trying to sell you on a position you don't really want. When considering your requirements, think about non-negotiables like location (onsite, remote, hybrid), pay range, title, type of company, seniority level, work authorization options, etc. When presented with a role from a recruiter or a job alert email, look for these key requirements first. If they don't align with what you want, chances are this isn't the position for you, and it might not be worth taking a phone interview. You may receive enticing emails from recruiters who present job opportunities as a shiny new toy. Recruiters try to highlight what they believe to be, or what other employees believe to be, the most attractive qualities about the job or company. These are essentially marketing emails targeted to the prospective hire, to grasp your attention, initiate a response, and convert you to a lead. But keep in mind, recruiters aren't mind readers. What's important to you is not public knowledge, unless you make it public. There are a couple of ways to engage with recruiters about your must-haves.

One option is to list your qualifiers right on your LinkedIn profile, especially if you're looking to do something slightly different like a new title or career change. We see this often on the talent acquisition side, and providing this kind of transparency upfront is extremely effective! When I'm sourcing for candidates online, of course I'm looking at all the job history, skills, experience, etc. But I'm also looking for any specific callouts that candidates included about their requirements. On your LinkedIn profile, remember there are a few places you can add custom text, like your main headline or the 'about' section. Let's say I'm recruiting for a company who is only open to hiring candidates into full time, direct hire positions. When I come across candidate profiles that indicate "only looking for a corp to corp (C2C) position", I know that individual is only considering contract opportunities, where they can be employed through a third party. Right away I know it's not worth either of our time to send a message, regardless of how perfect their experience might be. You can use similar disclaimers for job titles, job functions, career changes, company values - whatever is most crucial for you. Here are some general examples:

- "Established business analyst looking for a product owner role"
- "Experienced people manager seeking director management roles only"
- "Looking for visa sponsorship for employment"
- "Executive assistant currently completing a PMP certification, ready for my next challenge in project management"
- "Healthcare professional looking for an employer who value diversity, equity and inclusion"
- "Senior software engineer with aspirations to gain professional AWS or Azure cloud experience"
- "Music producer turned copywriter, seeking advertising agency positions"

I've also seen candidates include very direct callouts to recruiters, with specific instructions for contacting them:

- "Recruiters please send job description in your message"
- "Only looking for positions above 100K"
- "Remote-only, not willing to travel or relocate"

Including something like this on your profile will help deter recruiters from contacting you about positions that you're not going to want. You could also share your qualifier list with recruiters upon receipt of their InMail, almost like a "request for information" (RFI), for you to consider their proposed opportunity. Explore setting up automated responses from your inbox if you'd prefer a very passive approach. I've also seen candidates use third party tools such as free surveys or form builders, which allow users to create a mini "application" of their own! Candidates can respond to recruiters with their link and ask them to fill out the answers to their questions about the role. You can use a similar method for scheduling interviews as well. There are tools that connect to your calendar and provide a link for others to view your availability and book a meeting. Some of the most popular tools are Calendy and Microsoft Booking. They require a bit of setup on your end but are free to use and very convenient for sharing availability with recruiters.

SIGNING UP FOR JOB EMAILS

Most passive job seekers want to avoid searching through hundreds of positions every day. So why not have the positions come to you? Upload your resume to niche job boards or job aggregators and sign up for automated job listing emails that fit your job criteria. You'll get automated emails from multiple sources with lists of suggested positions when they are posted. It's a great way to stay up to speed on new positions on the market, without having to spend hours online sifting through pages of job listings. All will have the option to unsubscribe as well, so if you feel like you're not seeing the right types of positions, you can remove yourself from the email distribution list. For passive job seekers, I'd recommend looking at weekly or bi-weekly job listing emails, instead of daily. That way your inbox won't be flooded with emails, but you'll still have a regular cadence of opportunities to check out so you're aware of what's on the market.

USING STAFFING AGENCIES

Another reactive approach is to sign up with third party recruiting agencies that specialize in your industry. Most search firms are free for candidates, and only charge fees to the employers that hire them to assist with recruiting. Be warned, this may result in a flood of emails and/or calls from those firms, depending on your requirements and the structure of the staffing agency or search firm. It will likely require a little bit of time and effort upfront, but once you're "in" the database, those search firms are going to contact you whenever they have something you might be a fit for. Take the time to chat with one of the recruiters, set expectations on how much communication you'd like, and ask questions about how they work with clients. Search firms tend to have a bad rep because of the massive email distribution lists, and/or lack of response from the recruiters who work there. It's not a perfect system, but if you are looking for someone else to do the search work for you, that is exactly what search firms provide.

Third party recruiting agencies sometimes have access to confidential roles as well, that aren't posted anywhere online. This could be due to a replacement search, lack of internal recruiting support, or a special relationship/contract that the firm has with that company. Which means you'd have the inside scoop on positions that aren't available to the general public. Some staffing agencies also proactively pitch candidates to companies if you agree to be represented. This is a sales technique used by recruiting firms to showcase to clients the amazing talent that they represent, in hopes of gaining that company's business. This can work out really well for you if your profile catches the attention of a hiring manager. The recruiter will contact you to share more about the company and the hiring manager's interest, and you might be one of the very first people to interview for a role that hasn't been posted yet.

Chapter 6

Networking

Networking is extremely beneficial when looking for a new job. A CNBC article from 2019 shared a research study that supported "80% of jobs are filled through personal or professional connections". In my personal experience, that statistic seems a bit high. I'd estimate closer to 30-40% based on recruiting metrics I've reported in past roles, but of course each company and industry is different. However, it doesn't discount the fact that networking can help your job search in several ways.

First and foremost, connecting with your network uncovers positions that are not publicly posted, or ones that aren't posted yet. This greatly increases your chances of landing that role, since you wouldn't be competing against a massive applicant pool. Networking with former peers or managers can also lead to recommendations on social platforms, references, or letters of recommendation. By connecting with peers in your field, maybe folks who you know loosely but not closely, you can reassess your own qualifications. What skills and qualifications do your peers hold in similar careers? Do you think there are any skills you're lacking, or any areas with room for improvement?

Knowing what others can bring to the table, might encourage you to seek additional skills or training, to make your qualifications more robust. Finally, you could meet a mentor who is willing to offer guidance and advice to you throughout your career!

A good strategy for networking is to make a list of your personal and professional connections. Think about past coworkers or managers that you had a good relationship with. Also consider people you know through personal hobbies, classes, neighborhoods, or community groups. Do you know what these people do for a living? Chances are they're on LinkedIn and you can quickly find them and connect!

Check out digital platforms for community groups in your career field as well. Some options to explore include LinkedIn, Slack, Github, Meetup, Facebook, Shapr, Reddit, and Twitter. Twitter has become an increasingly popular space for recruiters to reach out to passive talent, especially recruiters from large global organizations. Some community groups posts jobs, others focus on engaged discussions around best practices and trends in your field. Recruiters sometimes check to see what groups candidates follow, so it's beneficial to get involved in a broader community. If you come across certain individuals in this group who are particularly engaged, or willing to offer their advice and support, add them to your connection list.

Once you're connected, or if you're already connected, reach out with a personal message. You don't want to blatantly ask for a job, but consider asking for advice, or information about what they do or the company they work for. Be authentic, and genuinely curious. Networking is all about building and deepening relationships. Here are some examples of messaging you could use:

-       "Hi [name], hope you're doing well. Not sure if you remember me but we took class together at [school]. I just came across your profile on LinkedIn and saw that you work for [company]. How do you like it there? I'm starting to look for new opportunities and [company] seems like a cool place to work! Any pros or cons you can share? Thanks!

-       Hi [name], great seeing you last month at the bowling league! I had no idea you worked in Geology...so crazy I'm in the same field. I'm in a Geographer role now but really interested in getting into Geoscience. Do you have any advice for getting into a Geoscientist role? I'd really appreciate any tips on skills I can work on, thanks.

-       Hi [name], it's been so long since we worked together at [company], how have you been? I see you're working for a healthcare company now, how do you like it compared to financial services? I've been thinking about switching things up myself, so just hoping to learn more about some other industries. Let me know!

-       Hi [name], we haven't met but we're both part of the [group name] on LinkedIn. I was really inspired by your post about the lessons you've learned in your logistics career! I'm just starting out in facility operations myself, do you have any advice for job seeking in this industry? Thanks in advance.

Of course there are also the more "traditional" networking methods available such as attending networking events, industry conferences, local community events, competitions, etc. You can find a ton of these options simply by researching these items with a keyword related to your career or industry. Face to face interaction does help make long-lasting impressions, but face to face events aren't for everyone. Digital networking might be a better option if you consider yourself an introvert, or if you have a hard time striking up conversation naturally when you're on the spot. Also, many of these events charge expensive fees, or require travel to another location. Whichever methods you choose, incorporating networking into your job search will add some surprising twists and turns to your job seeking journey!

Chapter 7

Resumes

Whenever you begin job seeking you should always update your resume. Not only is a resume required for pretty much all job applications, but recruiters will ask for one if they reach out to you proactively. It's always a good idea to have one ready to send. A resume is your strongest marketing tool, so it's important to cover the essentials.

Here's the basic checklist:

Work history

Contact info

Education

Skills and qualifications

Applicable certifications

A brief objective - i.e. what you're seeking in your next career or in your next company.

There are a few items you need to make sure are absolutely accurate. These include dates of employment at each company, clarity around level of education completed, and mentions of certifications or completed courses that apply to the work you do, outside of traditional education. Why is this important? If a company requires a background check, resumes are often used by HR teams and third-party providers as a source of truth. So, if there are discrepancies between what shows on your resume, and what comes back on the background check, that could potentially impact your employment.

If you have short gaps in employment, don't worry too much about carving those out specifically. You might even consider including the years of employment instead of month by month. Recruiters aren't typically concerned with short gaps. Life happens - you could have been in between jobs, or taking a long vacation, or taking care of a sick family member, or having a baby, etc. Larger gaps of employment however, around one or two years or greater, are more of a concern. In constantly evolving industries like healthcare, science, technology, or insurance, being two or more years away from the industry can affect your qualifications, as you might not be up to speed on current requirements and trends. If you do have this type of employment gap, I recommend adding a short explanation on your resume, so recruiters understand the reason behind it. If you completed some kind of coursework or education during that time to stay current with your industry, or to learn new skills, you should definitely include that.

While you don't have to include your full address, I still recommend listing the general region (city, state, province, etc.) as some employers can only consider candidates in specific locations, and you certainly don't want to waste your time. If you have plans to relocate, include a brief sentence about where you live now, where you're moving, and when. This will provide clarity for recruiters who have specific location requirements for hiring. Remember that recruiters are viewing hundreds, sometimes thousands of resumes for open positions. The first step of screening is weeding out candidates without the must-have requirements for employment. Before they even look at your skills and experience, they're going to check for things like location, work authorization, and required level of education (in some cases).

FORMATTING YOUR RESUME

Spelling and grammar are extremely important. On multiple occasions, I've witnessed hiring managers pass on a candidate because they didn't take the time to correct spelling errors on their resume. In a way, it can suggest a lack of attention to detail or unwillingness to put in a bit of extra time and effort. Which aren't exactly highly sought after qualities. If you're using a word processor like MS Word or Pages, there's a built-in spellcheck and grammar check function. I always recommend building your resume in a word processor first, so you can check for errors, then export it as a PDF. PDFs are the safest way to ensure your resume will upload correctly into any system, without any weird font or formatting changes. I've seen hundreds of resumes that look really wonky when they are uploaded into recruiting tools. This is due to the parsing function that most platforms use, to automatically import the content. If there are fonts, special characters, or formatting used in your Pages or Word document, that don't translate properly when parsed, the resume will not appear the same as your original. The text might bleed over into other lines, or overlap in front of tables, graphics, or punctuation. If a resume is illegible, it gives recruiters only two options. They can take the time to search for you on LinkedIn or some other platform to see your job history, or they can simply reject you for the position because they're unable to view your resume and qualifications.

For length, the rumors are true, a one-page resume is ideal. However, you may want to consider a short version and a long version to share more details when and if you feel it will be beneficial for specific types of positions. You might think you can't fit everything on one page, but you'd be surprised at what formatting can do! Tip number one, decrease your font size. In my previous career in advertising, we used a 6-point font size for small disclaimer text. If you're using a 9-point font or above, it will still be perfectly eligible on paper, you don't need to use the default 12-point font that most word processors have. You can also try playing with smaller margins, adding tables or columns on the side to include your skills and education sections, and put contact info in the header/footer. If formatting and/or proofing isn't your thing, you can hire an hourly resume writer to format or write your resume from scratch or edit/proofread your resume for mistakes and/or lack of clarity. You could also ask a friend or family member for a second pair of eyes if you don't want to pay for a service.

THE CONTENT

Now let's talk about the content, the meat of your resume. As mentioned above, I recommend having a couple different versions of your resume. Let's say you're considering two or three different kinds of roles because you have a variety of experience. Consider having one version that leans towards certain job titles and functions, and another version that's better for a slightly different role. Choose carefully when applying to jobs, to use the resume that puts your best foot forward.

Example. You are a tenured writer with many years of experience writing both internal and external communications for various companies. You've written just about everything under the sun - emails, marketing collateral, newsletters, web copy, social media content, intranet content, industry reports, case studies, employee spotlights, press and news releases, etc. However, some of the positions you've held primarily involved developing public relations campaigns, crafting press releases, and responding to information requests from the media. You're open to either type of role because you equally enjoy the work in either position. Create one resume that categorizes you as a "writer" or "communications professional". Include the type of content or deliverables you were responsible for writing, the audience you wrote for, which writing/editing styles you used, etc. Then, create a second resume that highlights your experience as a "PR professional" or "public relations specialist". This should include writing experience as well, but you'll emphasize specific public relations tasks, experience, and connections with various media outlets. Maybe you share some data points on successful press release campaigns. If you're applying to an internal communications role, it would make sense to use the first version. If you use the second, the recruiter reviewing your qualifications might assume you are only experienced in public relations, and inexperienced with writing internal messaging targeted towards an employee base. In the opposite scenario, if you are applying to a PR firm and you use the resume that is targeted to your PR experience, you're more likely to get a call than if you were to submit the standard writer resume. The recruiting team might be viewing hundreds of resumes for this role. They're going to shortlist the resumes that have public relations experience clearly listed, over general communications or writing experience.

Another route is to create a short, condensed version of your resume, and a longer version with more context, keywords, and deeper explanation of experience. If there's a particular role you see that is extremely relatable to a specific project or past role or yours, having that context on your resume could be your ticket in for an interview. If your resume leaves too much to be desired, it will be difficult for the recruiting team to determine if you have the qualifications, experience, and skills to be successful in that role.

For this example, we'll use Human Resources. You've spent 10 years in HR across many different industries. You've been tasked with a large variety of responsibilities including payroll, employee relations, exit interviews, compensation benchmarking, benefits and policy development, recruitment and talent acquisition strategy, workplace safety, and most recently, organizational development and training. You've really enjoyed the organizational development space and you'd like to get into a role that's more focused in that area, but you'd also consider an HR Generalist position. Your shorter resume should nicely summarize your wide breadth of experience across HR with a few key highlights for each role. It's clean, short, easy to read, and clearly articulates your career path and experience. You can use this as your go-to resume for all HR positions you apply to. Then, you build a second more robust resume, tailored to your experience with organizational development and training. Maybe this resume is a bit longer (1.5 to 2 pages). In the roles where you had organizational development tasks, add some detailed bullets highlighting those projects. Additionally, think back to previous roles where you might have done some similar type of work. Perhaps you didn't have an official title pertaining to organizational development or training, but as an HR Generalist you spent a significant amount of time training employees and leadership on new policies or benefits tools. Including these types of callouts in addition to your other job functions, is going to help your resume stand out. If you come across a position that is tailored to organizational development and training, use your longer resume. Again, recruiters are reading through resumes to determine how much of your experience matches the job qualifications. The easier you make it for recruiters to connect the dots, the more likely you'll be to receive an interview.

If you're wondering how to break down your work experience, here's a tried-and-true format. It's essentially positioning your experience in a case study structure: Challenge - Solution - Results. Think about some of the projects or initiatives you took on in a former role. What were you tasked with and why? What was the problem that needed to be solved? What was your solution? What did you build? What actions did you take? And finally, what was the result? How did your solution impact the business or the problem? When referencing the results, try to include tangible facts or data that inarguably provided value or improvements. Strong examples backed by data on a resume can sometimes encourage recruiters to override other requirements like number of years of experience, or specific industry knowledge. Early career professionals or recent graduates can use this format too. By reflecting on class projects or challenges you faced while in school, you'll find this structure really helps fill out your resume with more content.

KEYWORDS

I'd like to address one myth about recruiting. A lot of people think resumes are scanned by bots or ATS tools, searching for a plethora of keywords, and automatically reject profiles without those keywords. This is totally false. ATS platforms, applicant tracking systems, are enabled at most companies, but they are primarily used for storing and organizing candidate information, scheduling interviews, communication, etc. In reality, human recruiters are physically reviewing all resumes and applications. There's a great podcast by 'Get Hired with Andrew Seaman' that explains this: "In the US, it's legally required that every applicant who meets the qualifications for a role gets their application read. This is because of the Equal Employment Opportunity Commission (EEOC), which enforces anti-discrimination laws in the hiring process." It's important to understand the truth behind this misconception, because you don't want to blast your resume with 1,000 relevant keywords for no reason. Remember your resume is a marketing tool, it should be articulate and easy to understand. It's better to use job-specific keywords on your professional social profiles, like LinkedIn, where keywords are scraped and discovered using filters and other algorithms like Boolean search strings. In those cases, keywords certainly matter. Now this doesn't mean you shouldn't include some top keywords in your resume. Just make sure they're worked into the content in a way that makes sense, not smashed into a massive paragraph or listicle at the top. Also, by adding unnecessary keywords, your resume might be way too long. Personally, when I see 5–6-page resumes, it's quite overbearing and I often find it's difficult to navigate and find the information I'm looking for.

The only situation where algorithms or bots are used to filter resumes with missing keywords, are AI assisted platforms built for the purpose of screening resumes. One example of this is ZipRecruiter. You'll notice that I listed ZipRecruiter earlier as a go-to job aggregator platform.

ZipRecruiter is great for the purpose of viewing hundreds or thousands of jobs pulled from company websites. However, its value to paid-membership employers, is that it acts as an AI-assisted recruiter to screen resumes and/or only share resumes that qualify for the employer's open position. In this case, the technology used in the platform will screen your profile/resume for specific keywords and qualifications, which might not work to your benefit. However, as I've mentioned before, and will cover more in the next chapter, applying directly on the company website will bypass the filtering technology that lives within ZipRecruiter. If you're worried about bots rejecting your resume due to lack of keywords, you should only use tools like ZipRecruiter to view job listings, not apply to them. Apply on the company website instead, you know your resume is going directly into their ATS to be reviewed by an actual human on the recruiting or HR team.

TELL YOUR STORY

To sum it up, your resume should tell a story, not only your career story, but what makes you unique! If you're a career changer or went to school for something completely different than what you do now, include some of those details. It adds personality, uncovers common interests, encourages curiosity, and shows tenacity and ability to learn and grow. Tidbits of personal information on resumes can also be excellent conversation starters, which can lead to pleasant, natural dialogues with interviewers. This applies not only to initial conversations with recruiters, but also with hiring managers or future peers who are part of the interview process. Have you ever experienced an interview process where you really connected personally with everyone, and almost felt like friends by the end of the experience? By sharing a little bit more about yourself as a person, beyond your qualifications for a role, you're more likely to connect on a deeper level with the interviewers. This not only increases your chances for landing an offer, but also increases excitement towards accepting the role. Building rapport during the interview process paves the way for smoother onboarding and team comradery.

Chapter 8

Applications

I get it, applying to jobs can be super time consuming and frustrating, especially when you're not getting the responses you expected. By doing some of the prep work we discussed in previous chapters, you'll save yourself time by only applying to roles that align to your priorities list.

When applying, make sure to follow instructions carefully. Answer screening questions honestly, and if you decide to have two versions of your resume, choose the resume that best suits the role you're applying to. I always recommend applying on a company's careers pages directly. A lot of job boards and aggregators end up redirecting you to the company website anyways, but others allow you to apply directly through the platform. We already talked a bit about ZipRecruiter, and how it handles your resume and profile. Other tools, like LinkedIn or Indeed, have an option called "easy apply". This is a quick, one-click button that sends your most recently uploaded resume to the recruiting team with nothing else. If you're trying to get your resume in front of as many companies as possible, this might seem like a great solution. But frankly, if there are a ton of easy-applies from LinkedIn, your resume might not make it past the recruiter's inbox or LinkedIn project. Basically it keeps the application within LinkedIn itself, which requires recruiting teams to review resumes via email, and choose to upload your information to their internal candidate tracking tool. You also don't want to miss out on an opportunity because your resume didn't upload properly, or it was the wrong version, or you missed some screening questions, etc. From a recruiting standpoint, I've definitely been in a position before where I have to quickly review 100 applicants for 1 role. If there's missing info or I can't read the resume, it creates an extra step for me to reach out for a new version. Many recruiters won't take the time to do that (it's the sad truth), or can't reach out at all due to illegible contact info.

Personally, when I post any role on LinkedIn, I opt out of the "easy apply" option for candidates, and direct them to our company careers page instead. That way all applicants that come in are entered into our system automatically and are presented with our mandatory prescreening questions. LinkedIn allows recruiters to add prescreening questions as well, but again there's really no way of knowing whether your application made it past that stage. Your resume could be buried in an email inbox, or even sent to the wrong email address if the recruiter doesn't have their corporate LinkedIn license set up correctly. By applying on a company's careers page, you'll at least know you're in their ATS. Even if this job doesn't work out, or you don't hear back, your resume will be searchable on their platform. Which means your information might resurface for a future role, in which case the company would be able to proactively contact you about a new position.

If you're worried about companies keeping your resume on file, or if you'd prefer that your information is not stored for longer than your job search, there are privacy laws in place for that too. This concept has been more recently adopted in the US than in other regions like the UK for example, where it's been around a bit longer. But in 2023 there are more data privacy laws going into effect, especially due to some of the data breach situations that have transpired in the past couple of years. When applying to jobs online, or looking at a company website, you should be able to locate a privacy policy that discloses what companies do with your personal data. Many application forms also include a checkbox for your consent to have your information saved for a specified period of time. If you consent, you'll get a reminder when that period is coming to an end, at which time you can choose to keep your information on file, or have it removed from a company's database. Most large job aggregators like Indeed or Monster also have a privacy policy, so make sure you read through it and agree to the terms before uploading your resume to their database.

Checking out a company's career page is also a good way to make sure you apply for the role that is best suited for you. It's possible that one job posting caught your attention, but there's another role available that's an even better match. Recruiters generally know what open positions exist across the organization, but if you're applying to a really large company, recruiting teams can be huge and departmentalized. You'll want to speak with the recruiter who is handling the search for your top choice position. When in doubt, you can always apply to both. Some companies receive a ton of repeat applications consistently, and limit the number of jobs you can apply to to avoid duplication. So just be mindful of that if you decide to apply to more than one role. You might not be able to apply there again for a period of time, maybe 3-6 months or a year. Companies who have these limitations will list them publicly on their job site or notify you about this limit after you've submitted your first application.

COVER LETTERS

You might be wondering if you should include a cover letter with applications. In my opinion, you shouldn't. Adding a cover letter can be helpful, but it's not going to guarantee you an interview unfortunately. For some recruiters, a cover letter matters if you take the time to personalize it and highlight why you're interested in that organization or list the proactive steps you've taken to land that kind of role. You may be applying to a job that you're not 100% qualified for, but guess what, no one is 100% qualified. You never know if you will get a job if you don't at least apply. If you add a cover letter to provide context on where/how you can fill in the gaps, and if it falls in the right hands, it may work in your favor and land you a phone call. However, in full transparency most recruiters agree that a cover letter simply doesn't hold as much weight as it used to. If you Google "do recruiters read cover letters" you'll find a resounding "absolutely not" in results. In fact, a November 2022 Business Insider Instagram post, quoted a 10-year tenured Google recruiter, who recruits across the Middle East, Europe, and Africa. She recommended dropping the cover letter entirely and focusing on the resume. Her recommendations included making sure the resume is short (1 to 1.5 pages) clear and concise, and tailored to the job description itself.

An alternative option to writing a cover letter, is reaching out to the job posting owner on LinkedIn, or recruiting professionals at that company. A personalized message after submitting an application might do the trick, or at least help your name stand out among the long list of applicants being reviewed. Again, this is a suggestion that can work depending on the role and the person you contact. I've personally pulled some candidate resumes to the top of the list for phone screens, due to them messaging me on LinkedIn. A resourceful recruiter will review all communication channels, applicants, referrals, and sourced candidates equally and with a sense of urgency!

In a 2022 survey from a LinkedIn recruiter professionals group of 300K+ recruiters in the US, a question was asked: "What is the most important factor when considering new candidates for a role you're looking to fill?" 89% of survey respondents chose qualifications and skills. So, at the end of the day, Cover letters don't provide as much value as resumes. Your best bet is to ensure your resume highlights all your skills and qualifications, and update your LinkedIn profile to showcase the information talent acquisition teams need to evaluate your candidacy.

TRACKING APPLICATIONS

When you're in the application stage, think about how you're going to keep track of all the positions you're considering. If you're only using one tool, like LinkedIn for example, it will show you which positions you applied to, which are still accepting applications, which have been removed, etc. But if you are using multiple job boards and aggregators, it's going to be tough to keep track without capturing that list elsewhere. A basic excel spreadsheet is a solid option. At minimum I'd suggest including the title, job description link, company website, and when you applied. You could also try ranking them in order of interest before applying, so you can go for your top picks first. If you apply to a huge list of roles all at once, and hear back from everyone, you won't be able to fit in all the interviews in a timely manner. You can always go for your highest ranked position first and perform another search if those don't pan out. If you want to go the extra mile, you can include other sections in your tracker for notes during the interview process. Perhaps the hiring timeline, or number of interviews, or compensation or benefits info - basically anything you learn during your conversations with the company. By adding a data sort filter to your excel sheet, you can create an interest level scale of 1-10 or 1-5 for each position, so they can be auto ranked. This will especially come in handy if you end up getting to the offer stage with more than one company! Reviewing the pros and cons of each role and any associated ranking scales will help you make a final decision.

If possible, include the email address for your main point of contact as well. This will most likely be an internal recruiter or a third-party recruiter who introduced you to the company. If you need to follow up after an interview, or if you haven't heard back in a while and you want to understand what's happening, double check your list for the correct contact person.

This might seem tedious, but I have an interesting story that you'll be surprised to hear! I was once recruiting for a junior-mid level role, and we had one candidate who had already completed all interview rounds (candidate A). However, a newer candidate (candidate B) was two-thirds of the way there and the hiring manager was gravitating a bit more towards that person. We were able to buy time with candidate A, by explaining that we needed 2-3 more days to finish all final interviews before making a decision. 2-3 days was all that this candidate could spare, because they were considering another offer already and didn't want to lose out on that opportunity. I emailed candidate B asking to schedule the final interview asap so we could potentially have the option of hiring them, should that final interview go well. I got a quick response from candidate B saying that they were leaning towards another company/position and decided to bow out. Everyone was really bummed to hear this, as candidate B seemed to be the frontrunner. I was also shocked, since this candidate expressed a lot of interest in the role a few days prior. I called them to chat and understand where this pivot came from and left a brief voicemail. The next day, we were about 30 minutes away from making an offer to candidate A. Candidate B called me back, apologized, and disclosed that they had interviewed with another company where his main point of contact had the same first name as me! As soon as they saw my first name come through their inbox, they mixed up the two jobs/companies and accidentally withdrew from the wrong position. Candidate B was still very interested. They completed the final round that same day, and we ended up making an offer.

Now obviously this is a novice mistake that could have easily been avoided by paying more attention to detail. But it just goes to show you that when you're applying and interviewing for jobs, it can be really challenging to keep track of everything purely by memory. I've also had candidates email me with questions about verbiage in employee handbooks or non-competes after receiving an offer, except our company did not make them an offer…oops! Of course, I wrote back to make sure the candidate realized they had the wrong contact person, and wrong company. But it's a little unnerving to know that sensitive company information was mistakenly shared, by simply emailing the wrong person. Take the safe route, keep track of everything you need, and you'll avoid situations like this!

Chapter 9

Interviews

OK so you've heard back from a few companies, and you're about to enter the interview stage. While interview processes vary from company to company, most organizations have three major components to their candidate interview process: initial screening, assessment of qualifications (hard skills), and behavioral evaluation (soft skills). Now this doesn't necessarily mean you'll only complete three rounds of interviews. There is a possibility for multiple rounds within each of these stages, and/or multiple interviewers. Interview timelines vary from a couple of days to weeks to months, depending on the role, hiring timeline, and the weight or importance that role holds within the company.

INITIAL SCREENINGS

Your first interaction will likely be with a recruiter / talent acquisition professional or HR. This could be an internal recruiter at the company you're interviewing with, or a third-party recruiter who has been tasked with filling that company's position. Most of the time the initial screening is a short interview. You will discuss your background and experience, interest in the role, career aspirations, and learn more information about the company and the position. If you're an active job seeker who is considering many different opportunities, doing a lot of initial interviews is not necessarily a bad thing. Not only will you learn about different positions and career paths, but you'll also get a pulse for the market. Such as what kind of demand exists for your skillset, the general compensation ballpark offered, and an idea of the screening questions you'll be asked in the next interview. If you're more particular about your next role, or you simply don't have a lot of extra time, consider asking the recruiter some of your own screening questions before you agree to an initial interview. Doing a ton of initial phone screens can be draining and time consuming, so asking about compensation, or title, or work location, or whatever your priorities are up front, can save you from wasting your time.

It is a recruiting best practice to set expectations with you for the next round and/or your candidacy in general. Keep in mind recruiters are not decision makers (typically hiring managers choose who moves forward in the interview process). However, recruiters can and should at least give you an idea of the interview process, the timeline for hiring, and maybe even some of the top skills that make someone successful in this role! The interview process is key here. If you know what's coming, you'll have more opportunity to prepare. And the interview process itself may sway your decision to continue (or not) with this company. Ask whether there will be some sort of assessment of hard or soft skills, or a presentation, or a case study, etc. Or if it will be primarily Q&A style interviews. Are they done virtually or in-person? Who will you meet with in each round? Talent acquisition professionals generally know the interview plan for each role, so they should be able to provide you with this context upfront.

HARD SKILLS

Another stage of the interview process will focus on the qualifications and skills needed for the role, and how well you match up against that list. To prepare for these interviews you should read through the job description thoroughly and anticipate what questions interviewers might ask. If you know the names and titles of the folks you'll be speaking with, look them up on LinkedIn before the interview. See what kind of background they have or if you have any common ground.

Some companies use assessments during this stage, which could be an assignment that you have to prepare ahead of time, or a link to a knowledge-based quiz or evaluation with a specific timeline to complete. Other companies may do live whiteboarding or brainstorming sessions during the interview itself. These sessions require you to think on your feet and apply your knowledge real-time to a particular set of questions or scenarios. And some interviews will be strictly question and answer format. They ask you a very direct question, you answer that question to the best of your ability. If you don't know the answer, walk them through your thought process. Don't try to dance around or veil a response to make it sound like you know what you're talking about. It's more important to show how you think, how you solve problems you don't know the answer to, rather than knowing the answer. Remember, this is the "hard skills" interview, so the folks who are evaluating you likely have this experience and/or already know the answer. To put it plainly, they will be able to tell if you're qualified to perform in the role by the way you respond to their skill-specific questions.

This interview stage is also a good way to learn what a "day in the life" looks like for this role. Be honest with yourself. Is this something you'd be happy doing day to day? Do you feel like you have most of the skills and experience needed to be successful? Does this seem like the right career move for you now, or is it too much too fast? Or perhaps it's a step backwards?

Pro-tip: sending a follow up thank you email to the interviewers is a nice touch. It shows professionalism and a strong sense of interest. If you're selected to move to the next round, and for any reason you feel like the role is just not right for you, be transparent with the company and just let them know you're going in a different direction.

SOFT SKILLS

An additional stage of the interview process will focus on soft skills. Soft skills is a broad term, but generally speaking these interviews consist of behavioral or personality questions to get a sense for how you interact with peers, managers, direct reports, business leaders, etc. Behavioral evaluations also help companies understand how you react to specific scenarios, how you problem solve, and your approach to overcoming challenges or obstacles. Presentation and/or communication skills might be assessed here as well. Not every position requires you to present to others, or even interact much with others, so don't let this stage intimidate you if you consider yourself an introvert! However, it is important in any role to be able to communicate your ideas clearly. When faced with behavioral questions, make sure you understand them fully before responding. I've often experienced candidates who repeat questions back to me in a different way, to ensure they understand what information I'm looking for. When responding, take your time. There's nothing wrong with taking a minute to collect your thoughts, especially for scenario-based questions. Scenario-based questions typically drive you to reflect on a time where you encountered a certain situation. What was the challenge, how did you address it, what was the result? When answering these questions, walk them through your approach. You may think you know what soft skill the company is trying to "fish" for, but don't try to force your answer towards something you think they want to hear. Keep in mind that if you get this role, you will be held to an expectation to handle these situations similarly, so keep it real! If they're looking for something totally different, maybe this just isn't the right role for you, and that's OK too.

Some companies use online personality assessments for their behavioral evaluation. Typically, these are preconfigured surveys developed by psychologists to reveal behavioral traits, character tendencies, and motivators. Some common ones used by employers for personality evaluations include: Myers Briggs Type Indicator, GIANT Voice Assessment, Caliper Profile, HEXACO Personality Inventory, DISC Personality Test, and Eysenck Personality Inventory. The same rules apply here. Personality assessments are based on your own personal evaluation of yourself, so give careful thought into each question before selecting a response. These assessments can be kind of fun, as they may uncover some personality traits about yourself that you didn't know before!

POST-INTERVIEW QUESTIONS

At the end of each interview, you'll have an opportunity to ask questions. Here are some of my favorites that leave a great impression, and also provide you with some valuable takeaways:

Q: "How will success be measured in this role?"

• This shows employers that you recognize the importance of succeeding and bringing value to the organization. It also gives you a clear picture of the key performance indicators (KPIs) that you'll be measured against.

Q: "What will the first 30/60/90 days look like? And after 1 year?"

• Asking about structure and timeline shows that you take a strategic approach to your profession, and will also help you understand what to expect as you settle into your role.

Q: "What is a typical career path for this role? How does your organization support continuous growth?"

• If you plan to stay long term, you want to understand how this company supports upward mobility. At the same time, it gives the interviewers comfort in knowing you have interest and building and growing within the organization, verses hopping to the next job.

GENERAL TIPS FOR INTERVIEWING

Below is a short list of interview reminders, to help you prepare and move through the process smoothly:

- Be on time and prepared for every interview. A little online research on the company goes a long way! Especially researching the company's core values - this will come in handy during soft skills evaluations.

- Have questions ready ahead of time. As you go through the interview process, many of them will be answered, but you'll have an opportunity to ask questions at some point. Take advantage of that time to gather information on your top priorities.

- Ask about next steps and/or what the rest of the interview process looks like at every stage.

- If possible, try to find out what the hiring timeline is for this role so you have a realistic idea of when an offer could come (this will come in handy if you end up interviewing with multiple companies).

- Be mindful of how much time is scheduled for the interview. You and the interviewers should both respect each other's time and try to cover everything needed within the allotted interview timespan.

- DO NOT GHOST. Not showing up for an interview will most certainly burn a bridge with the company and/or the recruiter. You never know when you might cross paths with that person or another person within the organization again.

Chapter 10

Offers

Woohoo! This is the most exciting part. You hear from a company (HR, recruiting or the hiring manager) and they want to extend you an offer! Typically, you will have a verbal offer conversation before you get any paperwork. This is one of the moments where you can negotiate. Make sure you understand the whole package. This includes the base compensation, bonuses or commission and how/when that is received, out-of-pocket costs for health insurance, stock or investment options, and other perks like education/gym/cell phone reimbursement, etc. Does any of this information differ from what you expected during initial conversations? Do you feel like you've been lowballed? Or is the offer 100% perfect and everything you asked for...plus more? In any situation, keep your cool and ask questions to clarify anything in the offer that leaves room for interpretation.

If the offer isn't exactly what you wanted, speak your mind in a professional yet direct manner. Always thank them for the offer and the opportunity and remind them that you're still very much interested in the role and the company. When requesting modifications to your offer, directly reference where the offer fell short for you, and propose solutions to find middle ground. Negotiating is an art and it takes some time to master. Here are some examples of ways to negotiate during offer conversations:

- "Thank you so much for this offer, I'm really excited about this opportunity! However, when we initially spoke, I shared that my desired compensation range was roughly 10K higher than this offer. Can you help me understand how you landed on this number? I'd love to see if we can close that gap."

- "I really appreciate this offer and am excited to review the paperwork! However, my current package has a stronger PTO policy and 401K match. Are there any creative solutions we can explore to make this an easier decision?"

- "This is a great offer and I'm thrilled about the opportunity to join. I want to be transparent that I have another offer that's a bit more competitive. Could we talk about matching that offer, or perhaps a signing bonus?"

Once you have all the offer info ironed out, and you've received the paperwork, read through it carefully. It's important to understand the policies, out of pocket costs, benefits, and pay structure of your offer. You'll also want to make sure that what was shared with you verbally matches up against what is written in the offer. If you don't understand some of the verbiage, do not be afraid to ask questions. If you accept, you're putting your signature on a document for employment, and you're agreeing to the conditions of that offer. If your questions are related to specific items like employee policies, or noncompete agreements, or vesting periods for equity, you'll probably get the most value by speaking with the human resources team. I always tell candidates that I'm happy to share any knowledge I have about the role or the structure or the team, but that our HR team are the experts on policies and benefits.

Legally, recruiters cannot break down or explain contractual verbiage. They did not create the content of those contracts, and they're not lawyers, so they can't give you "legal advice". If you're in a situation where you don't feel comfortable signing an agreement because you don't quite understand the verbiage, it's recommended to have a personal attorney review the document before signing. Not all companies will not allow for redlines or alterations to the verbiage, even if that's what your attorney suggests. But using an attorney can give you peace of mind by explaining the potential outcomes of breaching that agreement. At least you'll know what you're signing, and what it implies.

DECIDING BETWEEN OFFERS

If you have more than one offer, weigh the pros and cons of the offers against your list of priorities that you established at the start of this book. As a refresher, this includes the compensation package, work location, job functions, company type / industry, company culture (specifically, the team you'll be on), and growth opportunities. The decision might be a no-brainer to you if you're really gravitating towards one of your offers. But if it's a really difficult choice, and more complex than simply comparing apples to apples, use data to help you decide! There is a weighted scoring matrix that some hiring managers and recruiters use to evaluate candidates post-interview. You can use this same method to evaluate your offers and use that data to help influence your decision. Here's how it works.

Take your list of priorities and give each of the six priorities a weighted scoring metric: i.e. 5 points for your top priority, 4 points for your second and third, 2 points for the next two, and 1 point for your least ranked (or some version of that). You can choose the weight per priority based on how important you feel it is for your next career. Then, go through the job opportunity and offer, and give each category a 1-5 score based on how much the opportunity fulfills that priority. For example, if the compensation is exactly what you wanted or higher, you might give that category a 5/5, but if it's lower than expected, you might give it a 3/5. If the company culture and team are amazing, give a high score. If it's a hybrid role and you were looking for something remote, maybe you give that category a 2/5. After you fill out all the categories, multiply the score by the weight, and you'll have a total weighted score for that particular offer. Here's a visual to help understand how this works:

(Weight)	Compensation: 5	Culture/ Team: 4	Job Functions: 4	Growth Opps: 2	Location: 2	Company Type: 1	(Weighted Score)
Company A	3	5	4	2	5	3	68
Company B	2	3	3	5	5	5	59
Company C	5	3	3	3	3	3	64

As you can see in this mock illustration, Company A ends up having the highest overall score. Even though Company C had the best compensation package, which was the number 1 priority, the it didn't average well across the rest of the categories. This certainly isn't meant to force your decision, but it can help you look at the entire opportunity from a more holistic and objective perspective.

MANAGING OFFER TIMELINES

Now let's say you don't have more than one offer yet, but you're expecting a second offer and you need a little more time to decide. Offers usually include a written date indicating when you need to respond. It's not uncommon to ask for an extra few days on your decision timeline. While it can cause a bit of discomfort from an employer perspective, they're not going to rescind the offer over a couple of days. They may, however, have a runner up option they'd like to offer if you do not accept. So just be mindful of that and respect their timeline as much as you can - it's a two-way street! By asking for that extra time, and having the company agree to it, you also create leverage for yourself with the second company. Reach out and explain that you have another offer already, and you have until "x" date to make a decision. This works to your advantage by putting some pressure on the second company to get your offer over the finish line, as they're now at risk of losing you.

It may seem strange to hear this from a recruiter like me! But in reality, it all boils down to transparency. As a recruiter, I'd rather know that my front-runner candidate is possibly going to receive another offer, so I can keep our runner-up warm. You shouldn't put all your eggs in one basket, and I promise recruiters won't either. You, the job seeker, should always choose the best opportunity for you, no matter what. Recruiters understand and respect that, and will do everything they can not to get blindsided or preemptively pass on someone else before getting official offer acceptance. Of course recruiters want the best possible candidate for the role, but sometimes timing doesn't allow for that. It's a common practice to have a backup pipeline of candidates who are nearly as qualified. As the weighted scoring matrix example showed earlier, sometimes the difference between a first choice and a second-choice comes down to an extremely small margin! So, if you find yourself in a reverse scenario, where perhaps you are the runner-up, don't take it personally. If a company makes you an offer, they're committed to hiring you because they are confident you'll succeed and bring value to the organization. Regardless of if you were the number two or even number three choice. We'll discuss more content like this about recruiter perspective, goals, objectives, and communication methods in the next chapter!

Chapter 11

Behind the Scenes

This chapter covers the steps that take place on the recruiting side. Every organization's structure is totally different, but understanding internal recruiting processes will give you a unique perspective during your job search. It will also equip you with new ways to interact with recruiters, hiring managers, and HR, to get the most out of your job seeking journey and hopefully land you a great job!

AN EMPLOYER'S FIRST STEPS

Let's start at the beginning, the part that exists before a job description even hits the market. Talent Acquisition, hiring managers, HR, and company leaders are all involved in hiring forecasting. This means there's a strategic plan and timeline in place to hire certain roles that require specific skills and experience/seniority levels. When companies are ready to hire externally, there's typically some kind of kick-off call or initial meeting to discuss the role. This call covers the job title, compensation range available, reporting structure, main responsibilities, hard skills required, soft skills required, timing, preferred background, etc. While some of this information is available in public job descriptions, recruiters will have additional information that is not listed externally. So, if you're interviewing with a recruiter, you might want to consider asking some of the following questions:

- Why are you hiring? Is this a backfill or a new role? Did someone leave due to the challenges of the role, or did they move into another role within the company?
- Is the company growing/expanding? Are there new initiatives or projects that require additional staff?
- What does the rest of the team or department look like? How many people are in this group and what do they do?
- Are there others in the role currently? (One of my favorite things to do as a recruiter is look at LinkedIn to see the backgrounds of other people who are currently in this role at the company. As a job seeker, you can do the same to get a feel for the type of backgrounds that translate well into this career path.)
- What is the timeline for hiring? Does the company need someone in this position for a specific project or quarter? Or is it more of the "when we find the right person" timeline? (This can help you gauge how much time you might spend in the interview process.)

THE RECRUITING LOOP

Once an organization is ready to go-to-market for a particular role, the job description will be posted. It's common to post open positions on the careers page of the company website, as well as job boards (niche or large scale). Some companies use paid social ads or email campaigns to spread awareness around their open positions. Simultaneously, the recruiting or sourcing team will begin proactively searching for and contacting candidates who fit the requirements. This is the beginning of what I like to call the "Recruiting Loop". The idea from a recruiting perspective, is to create a healthy pipeline of candidates. This is achieved by discovering candidates through multiple channels, including both active job seekers who are applying, and passive seekers who might not be actively looking, but are open to considering new roles that are a good fit. This is the period of time where you become discoverable. It doesn't matter whether you're an active or reactive job seeker, recruiters begin sourcing as soon as the position becomes available.

Now why is it called a Recruiting Loop? Talent acquisition teams are constantly focused on maintaining that healthy pipeline until the role is filled. If there is one thing I've learned from ten years of recruiting, it is a business of people, and nothing is guaranteed. Even if a company has three finalists for a role and ends up making an offer to all of them, there's always a chance no one will accept. That leaves the recruiter back at square one...unless they maintain a pipeline. So, most recruiting teams will begin conducting interviews as soon as they have some qualified candidates, while continuing to post, source, and interview new candidates periodically through the duration of the search.

TIMING AND METRICS

One of the most crucial performance metrics for recruiters is "time to hire", meaning the average number of days it takes to fill one position. According to 2022 LinkedIn data, the average time to hire ranges from 33 days to 49 days, depending on the skill set and industry. If you think about a typical interview process consisting of 3-4 rounds, you'd think that could be accomplished in a month or less, right? The vetting process can take a lot of time, and a lot of candidates before landing on the right person. It's fairly rare that the very first candidate who interviews ends up being hired. As candidates progress through the interview process, recruiters are getting feedback from hiring managers and interviewers along the way. This feedback allows them to better understand what background, experience, and personality is truly the best match for this position and company. Recruiters use that intel to go back to the beginning of the "loop", source more granularly, and evaluate new candidates against those adjusted requirements. This can happen more than once, creating a cyclical process that is constantly evolving while interviews are taking place.

You might be wondering why this information is important to you. Well, it's really to show that timing is not necessarily the most important thing when it comes to job seeking. The most important thing is finding the right person, or at minimum, finding a person in a timely manner, who substantially meets the requirements of the job. Just because a job has been posted for nearly 30 days, does not mean you shouldn't apply! Sometimes applying for a role that has been on the market for a while, is beneficial to you. The recruiting team will have a better understanding of the adjusted requirements for the role and will likely still be considering new applications at all stages of the process.

Now that doesn't mean you can't or shouldn't apply to brand new roles either. I'm certainly not encouraging anyone to wait to apply to something just because it's freshly posted - you don't want to miss a window of opportunity if you see something you really like! But keep in mind most postings expire at 30 days, or even 2 weeks in some cases. What you think is a brand-new role, might be a repost of the same job from several weeks before. And even if there are already candidates closing in on the final round, the company wants to hire the very best person for this role. If you're a good fit, many recruiters will help speed up the interview process to catch you up with the rest of the pipeline and timing of other interviews. So, the bottom line is that you shouldn't wait to apply to a role, nor should you be discouraged if a role has been open for a long time. Remember that recruiting is cyclical. If a company is 100% finished with recruiting, they will close the job posting. If the company is still accepting applications, that means they are still in the recruiting loop – aka interviewing and considering new candidates, regardless of how far along they are with others.

INTERVIEWING AT MULTIPLE COMPANIES

We discussed typical interview processes earlier in this book. As a refresher, there is usually a combination of initial HR or recruiter phone/video pre-screens, as well as 1-3 (or more) interview stages to evaluate core qualifications and soft skills. Asking recruiters upfront about the interview process and timing, will give you a better picture of how long your interview journey will last. This is especially important if you're interviewing with multiple companies at once. The most important thing about working with recruiters is transparency, but it's 100% a two-way street! You should be asking them questions about the process and timing, gathering as much information as you can, but also sharing back information about where you're at in your job search.

Let's say you're in the 2nd or 3rd round with another company, but you really like this new position and company that you just applied for and discussed with a recruiter. Make that person aware that you're on a tighter timeline, and they can use that incentive to help speed up your interview process. Ideally, you'll finish interviewing for all roles around the same time, so you can weigh the pros and cons of each. This will also give you a huge advantage when it comes to negotiating offers. If the recruiting team knows you are considering other opportunities, it won't be a surprise to them when/if you get an offer elsewhere first. And this is one of the biggest bargaining tools you have when it comes to offer negotiation. Again, transparency around your first offer can help a recruiter negotiate a stronger offer in hopes of swaying you to choose their company instead. Or, if you prefer to keep that offer information a little closer to the vest, you can also explain what kind of package would be powerful enough to sway you away from other suitors. Either way, you have an advantage because you are giving the recruiting team and hiring managers a baseline of the demand that you personally hold on the market.

Here's what happens on the recruiting side: a recruiter takes this information to hiring managers to encourage a timely and attractive offer for you. It is the goal of every single recruiter, to fill their positions with the best person possible - that is literally the primary task of a recruiter role. Now unfortunately recruiters don't own budgets for hiring, and ultimately the offer decision will be made by the business leader and/or hiring manager. But recruiters will do anything in their power to not lose an amazing candidate to another offer or company. Not only is it in everyone's best interest to hire the best person possible, but if a company misses out on hiring a great person due to timing or lowballing them with an unattractive package, the recruiter must continue to try to fill the role. Not filling a position quickly, or with the right person, directly affects their job performance and the amount of time they have available to work across all their other open positions. Selfishly, it's in the best interest of the recruiter to help you get to the finish line, to avoid having to start all over from the beginning. Help them help you! Being transparent with recruiters and vice versa, will make the process better for everyone.

LACK OF COMMUNICATION

The last item I want to touch on here is what I like to call the waiting game. How many times have you applied or interviewed for a job and then heard nothing back? Or maybe you went through to the final round, and now it's been two weeks and you haven't received any updates of any kind? I know, it sucks. And to be quite honest, there are a lot of recruiters out there who are terrible at communication. It's a bit of an industry flaw, and while I wish all recruiters were the same, chances are you will encounter some recruiters who update you every step of the way, and some who kind of leave you hanging. I'll also add that in many cases recruiters don't even know what to tell you, or when, because of lack of information provided to them internally. I'm not trying to make excuses for recruiters here, but I also know what it's like to feel the pressure of communicating with candidates when you have nothing to share, no updates, and no idea of when you will. It can be tough. I personally try to shed some light to my candidates no matter what. However, sometimes the information shared internally is not something we can disclose externally. So instead, we give a vague update that doesn't provide a lot of detail or clarity, but still gives you a touchpoint. This is what we call "keeping a candidate warm".

Now I can't promise you some secret technique for getting recruiters to update you, but I can share a bit about what might be happening behind the scenes, so you're better equipped with knowledge to influence your job seeking decisions. Below is a list of job seeking "ghost" scenarios you may encounter, with some possible explanations of what's happening on the recruiting or hiring side. Of course, there's always possibilities for something else, but at least you'll have an idea of what could be going on.

Scenario: You apply to a job online and you get a rejection email, but you don't know why.

- If this happens instantly or within a couple of minutes, it's likely related to a hiring requirement that automatically disqualifies you. Some examples would be your location, work authorization, or a must-have screening question that you answered in the application itself. It's possible that the company has an ATS with an automation workflow to reject anyone who doesn't meet basic hiring requirements.

- If this happens within a few days or weeks, it likely means the recruiting team reviewed your resume and determined you don't quite match the skills or qualifications needed for the job.

Scenario: You apply to a job online and you hear nothing back. Ever. Crickets.

(Recruiting best practices are to review every applicant, always, and either move them forward or send a rejection. Sadly, this doesn't always happen consistently.)

- The recruiter hasn't seen your application yet due to a huge volume of resumes.

- They're on the fence about your experience, so they put you in limbo without any communication.

• They have a healthy pipeline of candidates in the process already, and plan to return to the new applicant list only if their pipeline runs low.

Scenario: You have an initial pre-screen with a recruiter and never hear anything back, despite follow ups.

(Again, recruiters should be providing you with some sort of update, but if they're not, a few things might be happening.)

• The recruiter has not yet presented your resume to the hiring manager.

• The hiring manager is on the fence about your background and chooses to pursue other candidates first.

• There's a specific timeline for all pre-screens to take place, before anyone moves to the next round, so the company can evaluate and narrow down their options.

• There's an internal employee being considered for this role and the hiring manager must interview them before external applicants.

• There's a chance the position will be put on hold and recruiting has been asked to pause on interviews until it's resolved.

Scenario: You've made it through one or two interview rounds at normal pace, and now you're waiting patiently for a next step. You don't know where you stand.

• The recruiter is attempting to "catch up" other candidates to the stage you've completed, before the hiring manager determines who is moving to the final round, or to the offer stage.

• Someone, somewhere in the interview process, raised a red flag about your profile, and the hiring manager wants some time to consider whether this is a deal breaker.

• The company does not have a structured interview process mapped out, and the recruiter is unsure of what the next step should be.

• The recruiter is literally just waiting for the hiring manager, or the interviewers you spoke with, to provide feedback. (This happens often)

• There's someone else in the offer stage and they want to see how that plays out before they move you forward.

Scenario: You completed the final interview, and the recruiter told you they'd have a decision by a certain date. You're now past that date and wondering if you will be receiving an offer.

• The most likely situation is you are the runner up. The hiring manager decided to offer another candidate first, and your offer is contingent on the first candidate's acceptance or rejection. Most companies give a few days for a decision timeline on offers, but when negotiations come into play, this can stretch to 1-2 weeks before it's finally resolved. If you're considering other opportunities but you're still super interested in this one, my advice is to communicate your offers to the recruiter. Let them know the timeline you have to decide - this will create a bit of pressure on their end, and hopefully speed up the process.

• The company has a painfully slow approval process for offers. The recruiter and hiring manager have offer details pending but can't officially extend until they are routed and approved.

• The company had to reschedule some other person's final interview, which pushed the decision timeline back. They want to finish that interview before carefully deciding who to hire.

Conclusion

Let's recap what we've covered! Before diving into your job search, identify and prioritize what's most important to you in your next position. Compensation package, work location, job functions, career growth, culture, and company type. Use this list to approach how and where you seek opportunities. Take a bit more time upfront to be strategic about the jobs and companies you target, and you'll find better quality of positions vs a huge quantity of roles that end up being a waste of your time.

There are three different methods you can try for job seeking: The Company-First Method, the Job-First Method, and the Reactive Method. You may find one method to be more successful for you than the others, or you may find that certain methods work better during different points in your career. All the methods offer a systematic approach that can be applied any time you begin this process.

Remember, there are several things you can go back to reference in this book, including a list of digital platforms, job boards, and social tools used for hiring, and how employers and recruiting teams use them. You can also review the preparation tips for your resume, applications, interviews, and offer negotiations. Jot down or memorize some of the verbiage and questions that might be useful to you during your job seeking process. Now that you have the inside scoop on how recruiting operates, you'll feel more confident interacting with recruiters, interviewers, and hiring managers.

Job seeking can be a very satisfying process once you land the role you're looking for! Not only can you use these tips for your next job, but now that you've learned some new strategies, you'll be able to apply these tactics again in the future. One of the best practices to keep in mind during your search is to stay positive and know that there's always something new out there waiting for you. With the right preparation and mental attitude, you'll enter a new and exciting chapter of your career, and life!

Thank you for purchasing Recruitability! If you enjoyed the book, please leave a review on Amazon so other readers can benefit from this information as well.

Citations

Corporate Culture | Inc.com.
https://www.inc.com/encyclopedia/corporate-culture.html.

"Our Favorite Culture Tools." *Board of Innovation*, 20 Sept. 2022,
https://www.boardofinnovation.com/staff_picks/our-favorite-culture-tools/.

"Company Culture" | *Course Hero*,
https://www.coursehero.com/file/80928995/Company-Culture docx/.

"The Wonderful Company | Company Overview & News."
Forbes, Forbes Magazine,
https://www.forbes.com/companies/wonderful-company/?sh=3acb2b3b6f6f.

"Here's How Recruiters Read Resumes." *Andrew Seaman* |
https://podcasts.apple.com/us/podcast/heres-how-recruiters-read-resumes/id1609671453?i=1000595117827

"LinkedIn Usage and Revenue Statistics." *Mansoor Iqbal,* 31
Jan. 2023 |
https://www.businessofapps.com/data/linkedin-statistics/

"How to get a job often comes down to one elite personal asset, and many people still don't realize it." *Julia Freeland Fisher,* 14 Feb 2020 |
https://www.cnbc.com/2019/12/27/how-to-get-a-job-often-comes-down-to-one-elite-personal-asset.html

"Corporate Culture" |
https://feritotribunal.com/meri3188lah/Corporate-Culture.htm
l

"Scrum. A guide to scrum: what it is, how it works, and how
to start." *Atlassian* | https://www.atlassian.com/agile/scrum

Made in the USA
Las Vegas, NV
15 January 2024

84425384R00076